A TYPOLOGICAL GRAMMAR OF HO

Ⅰ. Foreword

This special issue of Research Series came about as the result of work that was undertaken by Dr. Koh for the plan of the institute since 2002. The research was planned with a deep approach toward the extension of South Asian Studies. In the available time, he was able to analyze the Ho language with the general heading of syntax and typology. Thus, I would like to express my sincere appreciation for his active and extensive research. This book provides a useful outline for Ho grammar with extensive examples. The whole subject is covered in 36 topics systemically arranged. Thus this research is organized not on a general grammar basis but by topic, so that salient theoretical issues may be discussed in a comparative context. At the same time a wealth of descriptive information is accessibly presented. Moreover, this book is the result of the author' s observations and analysis of original sources. Majority of examples cited by him are selected from the field trip over and over years. He has rendered an exceptional service to the field of tribal languages in India by making a survey that takes into account the research done in the extension of South Asian studies. It is a matter of regret that there has been no concerted effort to research on the tribal languages by Korean scholars. However, this book has made an attempt to document the typological and syntactic system of those languages and incorporate as many of the insights gained from recent research as possible in Korea.

Consequently, apart from looking at languages, our institute has also concentrated on other areas. Growing interests in South Asia has brought with the deep and extensive issues. Thus the research series in South Asian studies are to be published in different volumes demarcated by the following broad categories: (i) Introduction to South Asia, (ii) Language, (iii) Classics, (iv) Religion and Thought, (v) Humanities, (vi) Social Science, (vii) Translation. This measure of work represents a commitment to researches unprecedented in South Asian Studies.

Therefore, these researches on South Asia will be an invaluable resource for people and countries who have wished for a comprehensive book about this region.

Director

Prof. Choi, Jong-Chan

II. Preface

The purpose of this book is to provide a general and typological introduction of Ho language to a fascinating field for those who want to learn and understand it with the broader and deeper linguistic context. Before proceeding further, it is appropriate that we identify more precisely the language to be discussed. A brief survey of the Ho language in terms of historical background, number and region is therefore given here. Although this may not be necessary, it will be helpful to those less familiar with the language. Ho belongs to the Munda languages of the Austro-Asiatic language family spoken primarily in Jharkhand, Orissa and West Bengal of India by about 1,077,000 people. It is generally argued that the Munda languages and Dravidian languages were the first Indian language with which Indo-Aryan languages came in contact. Although Munda words are not as numerous as words of Dravidian origin, they are often names of common objects which are used in animal, bird, plants etc and hunt and so well assimilated as not to be recognizably foreign. Witzel (1999) also states that some Sanskrit words and prefixes are influenced or related with Proto-Munda languages. Thus, it is estimated that the Ho tribes resided in the Indian subcontinent before Aryan came to India.

Although with the help of the index, an overall basic

description of the each category may be extracted in terms of Greenberg (1968)' s aspects. Attempts to survey a field must still be selective, and even though an attempt has been made to cover all typological perspectives. Characteristics of the Ho language includes three grammatical numbers (singular, dual, and plural), two genders (animate and inanimate), a distinction between inclusive and exclusive first person plural pronouns, the use of either suffixes or auxiliaries to indicate tense agreement, and the use of intransitive marker as passive. Much of interest has no doubt been omitted and has been deeply researched. In general priority has been given to simple presentation of facts rather than to the different theoretical analyses with various examples. Ho language appears to exhibit a typological profile that is very different from that which is typical of the Mon Khmer languages to which it is related but these differences are not always attributable to Dravidian and/or Indo-Aryan influence. For example, the verb structure of the Ho language is extremely synthetic, indeed significantly more synthetic than structures typical of either Dravidian or Indo-Aryan languages. In this way, it shares certain structural affinities with so-called 'pro-drop' phenomena with the rich agreement. Thus in this book, we research on most of agreements which are related to the pro-drop phenomenon. This heavy 'pro-drop' language is due to the rich agreement attended by hierarchy. There is an attempt to show how subject agreement marker can be suffixed to preverbal constituent according to the concept of merge under minimalist program, and anti-symmetry. And there are some studies of the agreement patterns in Ho. And we also discuss that agreement marker also has extra functions and the relation between the occurrence of the agreement and thematic role in Ho. In other words, with regards to verbal and syntactic phenomena characteristic of Ho languages there appear to be systems of noun incorporation patterns that are highly marked or even unique. Another characteristic of the verbal systems of particular Ho language that is rare or unique among the world's languages is the agreement of a verb with arguments. Throughout the book, we also examine the relation between pro and the verbal reflexive and the properties of reflexives with passive since it is a crucial point to understand the nature of verbal reflexive in Ho. Thus this book brings us to the whole set of grammar of Ho coming under the general heading of syntax and typology.

Apart from these linguistic concerns, there is a different set of reason why Ho language merits attention. First of all, Ho presents special opportunities for the investigation for historical issue that Munda had influenced on Sanskrit either by words or prefixes.

Secondly, although its use is not considered to be in serious decline, the language is under-documented and therefore little known to the outside world. This book is to promote the documentation, maintenance, preservation and revitalization of the minor language through linguistic perspectives. And this book serves as a stepping-stone for making comparative study with other tribal languages. Moreover, not only is the historical importance relatively put, but the political and geographical issues are also fairly concerned since Ho may become a state official language of Jharkhand and it is spoken in the heart of iron mines.

It should be also added that this book involves essentially the presentation of various data through the field trip to communities to dialogue with speakers of Ho language in Jharkhand and Orissa. New data, however, keeps coming to light and new analyses keep appearing. It is impossible for a work to be 'complete' even in the sense of reflecting fully the state knowledge at the time of its publication.

I hope that readers will find this book useful, and look forward to their advice. Special thanks go to the institute and Prof. Choi who has provided these sheets. I am also grateful for my family.

Koh, Tae-Jin

Table of Contents

List of Abbreviations and Symbols

1	first person	**2**	second person
3	third person	**Abs**	absolutive
Acc	accusative	**AF**	actor focus
Apass	antipassive	**aux**	auxiliary
Caus	causative	**conj**	conjunctive
Dat	dative	**def**	definite
Erg	ergative	**f**	feminine
fut	future	**Gen**	genitive
imperf	imperfective	**ind**	indefinite
inf	infintive	**Infl**	inflection
Inst	instrumental	**intr**	intransitive
Loc	locative	**m**	masculine
mkr	marker	**n**	neuter
Nom	nominative	**Npst**	non-past
Obl	oblique	**obj**	object
Part	participle	**pass**	passive
perf	perfective	**PF**	patient focus
pl	plural	**pres**	present
pron	pronoun	**pst**	past
rel	relative	**sg**	singular
spe	specific	**spec**	specifier
sub	subject	**tr**	transitive
v	light verb	**Vol**	volitionality
Caus	Causative marker	**comp**	complementizer
VR	Verbal Reflexive	**VREC**	Verbal Reciprocal
[-TR]	Intransitive	**[+TR]**	Transitive
cp	Conjunctive Participle Marker		

A TYPOLOGICAL GRAMMAR OF HO

INTRODUCTION

The purpose of this grammatical sketch is to provide a brief description of the Ho language focusing on the typological characteristics of the language. As the language is a verb-final language, Ho shares a number of its grammatical features with other verb-final languages such as Hindi, Punjabi, Assamese, Telugu, Tamil and Korean. While providing the grammatical sketch, we will make statements that will show how this language is similar to or different from some of the selected verb-final languages on the basis of Greenberg (1963)'s universal grammar. Thus, for the sake of clarity this bookt has been divided into many sections. Moreover, we will also show some major features of Ho in terms of linguistic aspects such as agreement and verbal reflexive and etc in detail.

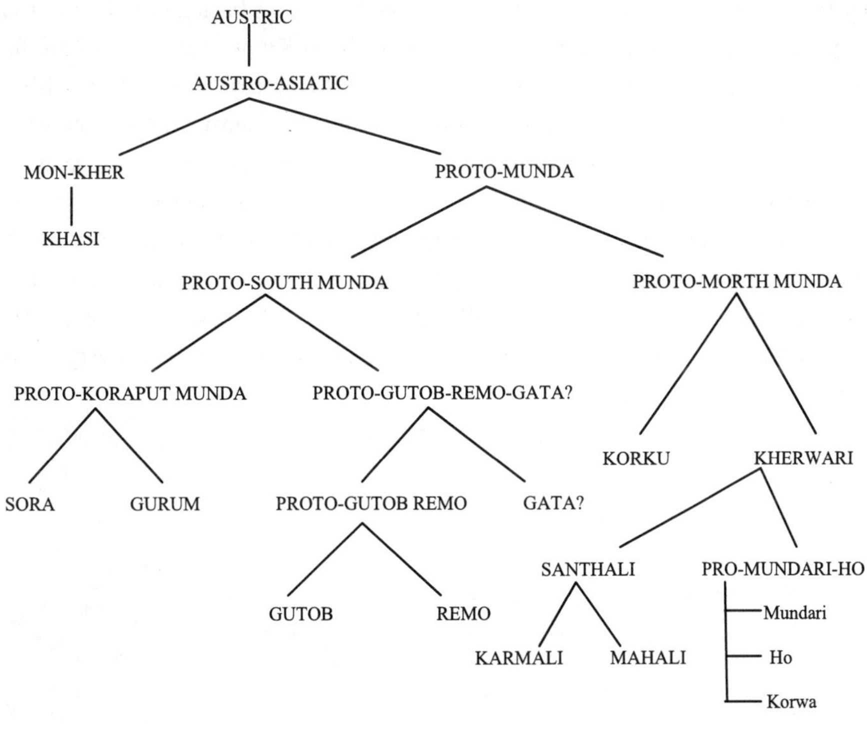

Ho is a language spoken by the Ho tribe in India. Ho is the name of a tribe, and the language is often called Ho–Kaji, that is, the language of the Hos. The word Ho is identical with *har* and *hara*, the words for 'man' in Santali and Mundari respectively. The native script of the language Ho is Warang Chiti or Varankshit. The other scripts of Ho are Roman and Devnagri. The Hos are concentrated in the Kolhan area of the Singhbhum district of Jharkhand, and are also distributed in the adjacent areas of Orissa, West Bengal and Madhya Pradesh. They were once known the larka kols. It is generally believed that the Ho language was classed for linguistic purposes as the Kolarian. Grierson (1967) has concluded, "The Mundas, the Mon-Khmer, the wild tribes of the Malay peninsula and the Nicobarese all use forms of speech which can be traced back to a common source though they mutually differ widely from each other". Now this mother tongue Ho is regarded as belonging to the Kherwarian group of the Austro-Asiatic family of languages. There is much controversy over the origin of the Austro-Asiatic language. Some named the Munda languages as Austro-Asiatic. Heine Geldern (1928) suggested that the Mongoloid people entered India from the north-eastern side and brought with them the Munda languages which later spread in middle India. But others opine that the Austro-Asiatic language was brought by the Kolarians through the west end of the Himalayas and by the Mon-Khmer speaking people from the east of the Himalayas. To the best of our knowledge Ho belongs to the Munda Branch of the Austro-Asiatic family. According to the 2001 census, 1,077,000 persons speak the Ho language. Moreover it is also generally believed that Munda languages including Ho and Dravidian languages were the first Indian languages with which Indo-Aryan languages came in contact. Although Munda words are not as numerous as words of Dravidian origin, they are often names of common objects which are used in the forest and hunt and so well assimilated as not to be recognizably foreign. Thus, it is estimated that the Ho tribes resided in the Indian subcontinent before Aryan came to India.

1. Basic word order

Greenberg (1966)'s Universal 7 illustrates that ' If in a language with dominant **SOV**, there is no alternative basic order, or only **OSV** as the alternative, then all adverbial modifiers of the verb likewise precede the verb '. Let us consider the following examples:

[1](1)	(añ)$_i$	uli–	iñ$_i$	jom–	ke-	D-	a
	I	*mango*	*I sg*	*eat*	*pst*	*[+tr]*	*dec*
	SUBJECT	OBJECT		VERB+AUX			

'I ate a mango. '

(2)	(añ)$_i$	hola	uli	-iñ$_i$	jom–	ke-	D–	a
	I	*yesterday*	*mango*	*I sg*	*eat*	*pst*	*[+tr]*	*dec*

'I ate a mango yesterday. '

(3)	(añ)$_i$	uli	hola	-ñ$_i$	jom–	ke-	D–	a
	I	*mango*	*yesterday*	*I sg*	*eat*	*pst*	*[+tr]*	*dec*

' I ate a mango yesterday. '

(4)	uli	añ$_i$	-^{y}o	-ñ$_i$	jom-	ke-	D-	a
	mango	*I*	*emph*	*I sg*	*eat*	*pst*	*[+tr]*	*dec*

'I also ate a mango. '

As illustrated above, the pronominal subjects are usually dropped due to the occurrence of the subject agreement marker. In unmarked sentences, the subject agreement marker occurs to the preverbal constituent in Ho. Munda languages as like Ho, Mundari, Santali have the most elaborate verb morphology. Their argument can appear as pronominal affixes in various ways. However, there is a restriction of the occurrence of the subject agreement marker when there is a scrambling between the subject and the object in Ho.

---

[1] The transitive simple past form *–keD-* is broken into *ke-* and *D* while the intransitive simple past form is -*ken* (*n* is an intransitive marker). We will discuss this point in detail later.

Ho is a nominative-accusative language like Assamese, Telugu and many Austro-Asiatic languages. By nominative-accusative type we mean that the subject is always in the nominative case and the object is in the accusative case. In general, the verb agrees with the subject in person, number and gender in case the language exhibits agreement in person, number and gender (PNG) in nominative-accusative languages. The subject in Ho is in the nominative case and the direct object is in the accusative case. However, Ho does not exhibit verb agreement with the subject like some Tibeto-Burman languages such as Manipuri, Tangkul, Angami, Rabha etc. For example:

Rabha (Tibeo-Burman language)

(5) nang sa-nO

you eat-FUT

'You will eat.'

Santali (Austro-Asiatic language)

(6) orak-iñ nel-a

house-1sg see-FIN

'I will see the house.'

However, the subject agreement marker also occurs to the end of the verb as a suffix as followings:

(7) (añ)$_i$ uli jom– ke- D- a -ñ

I mango eat pst [+tr] dec –1sg

'I ate a mango. '

Santali (Austro-Asiatic language)

(8) orak nel-a -ñ

house see-FIN-1sg

'I will see the house.'

In Ho, Mundari and Santali, the preferable position of the subject agreement marker is the preverbal constituent. Thus, the sentences (1) and (6) are more common than (7) and (8).

2. Personal Pronouns

In Ho there are personal pronouns of the 1st, 2nd and 3rd persons each in the singular, dual and plural numbers. And the dual and plural of the first person have separate forms used when the person being addressed is included and when he is excluded. And there is no distinction between 3rd person masculine and feminine. However, there is no corresponding form for ‘it’ in Ho. And the 1st, 2nd and 3rd person dual pronouns are also used as an honorific form of addressing one person.

There are eleven pronouns in Ho as illustrated in:

pronoun	**Singular**	**Dual**		**Plural**	
1 st	añ	Incl [+you]	alaŋ	Incl [+you]	abu
		Excl [-you]	aliŋ	Excl [-you]	ale
2 nd	am	aben		ape	
3 rd	ini$^{?}$(far) / a^{y}e$^{?}$ (near)	akiŋ / inkiŋ		ako/enko	

As illustrated in the sentences (9) and (10), the expletive pronouns are not present in Ho.

(9) nen- ta$^{?}$a isu rabaŋ- min- a

this near very cold is dec

‘It is very cold here.’

(10) puti tabul- re min- a

book table on is dec

‘There is a book on the table.’

Regarding to the agreement, each pronoun also has a shorter form, dropping the initial letter ‘a’ from the free form, to be used when the personal pronouns occurs as as subject agreement marker or as an object agreement marker. These forms are referred to as bound forms as following:

Agreement marker	Singular	Dual		Plural	
1 st	-ñ	Incl [+you]	-laŋ	Incl [+you]	-bu
		Excl [-you]	-liŋ	Excl [-you]	-le
2 nd	-m	-ben		-pe	
3 rd	-i(far) / -e(near)	-kiŋ		-ko	

(11) okoe dub-tan-a?

who sit-pres-dec

'Who is sitting?'

(12) okoeti-kin tingun-tan-a?

who-dual stand-pres-dec

'Who (dual) are standing?'

(13) okoete-ko tingun-tan-a?

who-pl stand-pres-dec

'Who (plural) are standing?'

The pronominal suffixes (agreement markers) referring either to the direct object or to the indirect object, they cannot co-occur together like Santali. And pronominal reference is restricted to animte beings. Because the distinction between animate-beings and inanimate- beings is important in Ho.

In So:ra: all nouns and noun equivalents, when used in the nomiative case, have ending *–n* or *–en*. Thus, all pronouns have ending *–n* in the nominative case. And there is no dual number except in the first person.

3. Possessive

Placing postpositions after the nouns denotes different cases, and such there is no suffixation process or declension in Ho. There is only one suffix, basically, to be used as a genitive marker for the noun and that is *-a*. And glottal sound comes to either left of the genitive marker or right of that marker when a genitive marker occurs after vowel.

Possessive	Singular	Dual		Plural	
1 st	añ-a	Incl [+you]	alaŋ-a	Incl [+you]	abu-a$^{?}$ / abu-$^{?}$a
		Excl [-you]	aliŋ-a	Excl [-you]	ale-a$^{?}$ / ale-$^{?}$a
2 nd	am-a	aben-a		ape- $^{?}$a / ape-a$^{?}$	
3 rd	ini-a$^{?}$ / a^{y}e-a$^{?}$	akiŋ-a		ako-$^{?w}$a / ako-^{w}a$^{?}$	

But a genitive marker *-a* is used for only animate nouns. Instead, *-ria* is used with the inanimate nouns.

[2](14) (añ)$_i$ am- a ote- ñ $_i$ nel– la- D- a
I you gen field Isg see ps.peft [+tr] dec
'I had seen your field. '

(15) pro a^{y}e- a$^{?}$ ote- ria da$^{?}$a ñ̃ $_i$ nel -a- -D -a$_i$
I He gen field gen water I sg see pst.pef [+tr] dec
'I had seen his field's water.'

---

[2] Here, the past perfect form is actually '*–la*'. But '*l*' becomes weak because of the coalescence with the preceding consonant *–l*. In Ho, we can find lots of cases when *-l* is followed by a nasal consonant.

Here we can see that the genitive precedes the governing head noun in Ho like most of verb-final languages as Greenberg (1966) stated in his universal 5. And there is one more genitive marker, that is *-te-* for 3rd person. However this 3rd person genitive marker occurs to the right of the head noun as followed in[3]:

(16) bau - te
elder brother his
'his elder brother'

(17) unDi - te
younger brother his
'his younger brother'

(18) era -te
wife his
'his wife'

And 3dr person genitive marker *-te* can be also used with 3rd pronominal possessives as followed in:

(19) $a^{y}e$ -$a^{?}$ bau -te
he gen E.Bro his
'his elder brother'

(20) ako -$^{w}a^{?}$ bau -te
they gen E.Bro his
'their elder brother'

(21) añ- a- bau – (*te)
I gen E.Bro his
'my elder brother'

(22) ape- $a^{?}$ bau (*te)
you gen E.Bro his
'your elder brother'

And there seems to be no distinctive possessive pronouns. In Ho the possessive and the possessive pronouns are homophonous. In Ho possessive pronouns are also formed by suffixing *–ta-* followed by the shortened forms of the personal pronoun to the animate or inanimate obeject possessed. These compound forms are very common (Burrows 1980).

3 This case may support that Ho used to be SVO language.

4. Order of indirect object and direct object

The indirect object precedes the direct object in unmarked sentence. In Ho, both the dative case marker and the accusative case marker are not actually present. However, the postposition *–ta$^{?}$a-re* 'to'is often used as a dative case marker to distinguish between the direct and the indirect object.

[4](23) (añ)$_i$ (am)$_j$ mi^{y}ed uli– iñ$_i$ em– a– m$_j$ –tan –a

I you one mango Isg give epen IIsg prog dec

'I am giving one mango to you. '

(24) pro$_i$ am̃- ta$^{?}$a minDo kui-hon-ko$_j$ kul- keD- ko-$_j$ wa- ben$_i$

you(pol) me near one girl pl send pst 3sg dec 2dual

'You sent girls to me.'

In Indo-Aryan and Dravidian languages indirect object and direct object can be freely scrambled. In contrast, in Ho, the direct object can precede the indirect object if and only if the indirect object is lexically Case-marked as in (25).

(25) (añ)$_i$ mi^{y}ed uli$_j$– iñ$_i$ (am)$_j$ em– a– e$_j$ –tan –a

I one mango Isg you give epen IIsg prog dec

'I am giving one mango to you. '

Recall that the distinction between animate beings and inanimate beings is important factor in Ho. When a noun denoting an inanimate object stands at the diect object of a transitive verb, the 3rd pronominal agreement marker *–e* is inserted into the [–past] tenses. However, in [+past] tenses, that marker cannot be inserted into the verb. And as I already mentioned earlier, both direct and indirect object agreement marker cannot occur together. Thus, when the indirect object is not lexically case marked, the direct object agreement marker cannot occur but the indirect object agreement marker occurs, and when the indirect object is lexically case marked, the direct object agreement marker can occur.

---

[4] The vowel *–a-* between *em* 'give' and *m* '2nd sg Agr' is the epenthesis. We will see more examples in 'morpho-phonemic change' section.

In Ho the auxiliary verb follows the main verb like in all other verb-final languages. Thus, the order of the constituents is Verb (V) + Auxiliary (AUX).

(26) pro_i pro_j nel-keD-iñ$_i$-ya-m$_j$

you me see-pst-1sg-dec-2sg

V + AUX

'You saw me.'

Scrambling is not permitted in Rabha if the subject and the direct object are not case-marked as the followings:

(27) tupu llbak mOnOk -a

snake frog swallow-PRES INDEF

'A snake swallows a frog.'

(28) *llbak tupu mOnOk -a

frog snake swallow-PRES INDEF

'A snake swallows a frog.'

The sentence is ungrammatical in the intended sense. It has the interpretation that the frog swallows the snake. The reason for the nonpemissiblity of scrambling is the absence of the lexical case marker *–be* with *tupu* 'snake' and *–nga*, the accusative case marker with the DO *llbak* 'frog'. Ho which does not have both the accusative and dative case marker (although *-ta$^?$a-re* can be used as a dative case marker), also has the restriction of scrambling. We will see in detail in the agreement section.

5. Postposition

Ho has postpositions that follow the noun like all South Asian languages which are +VF languages. So Ho is also Head final language in terms of the position of the adposition and the verb. All the South Asian languages except Khasi have postpositions.

(29) owa$^?$ - re

house *in*

'In the house '

By adding locative postpositions to the demonstrative pronoun we get locative adverbs as in the following examples:

(30a) nen -re/-te	(30b) en -re/-te	(30c) okon -re/-te
this *in*	*that* *in*	*which* *in*
'here'	'there'	'where'

According to Neukom (1998), postpositions are distinguished from case markers by the fact that they are bisyllabic independent words, whereas case markers are monosyllabic and need to be attached to a host in Santali. Unlike Santali, Ho has both monosyllabic as well as polysyllabic postposition (compound postposition) as the followings:

(31) ha$^?$tu -rea$^?$ Owa (Burrows:1980)

village-of house

'The houses of the village.'

While *–a$^?$* is used for animate beings, *-rea$^?$* is the form of the locative Genitive of inanimate nouns only in Ho.

6. Position of the auxiliary verb

According to Greenberg (1966) universal 16, it is argued that '… in languages with dominant order SOV, and inflected auxiliary always follows the main verb.'

The auxiliary verb follows the main verb. In (24) above the transitive simple past tense marker *-keD-* and the declarative marker *-a* follow the verb stem *kul* 'send'.

(32)	pro $_i$	laD-	iñ $_i$-	jom-	dai-	a
	I	*bread*	*I sg*	*eat*	*can*	*dec*

'I can eat bread. '

In (32) we also see that a modal auxiliary *dai* 'can' follows the verb stem *jom* 'eat'.

7. Comparison

The marker of comparison *–te*$^{?}$*/-ete*$^{?}$ follows the standard of comparison in Ho like in other verb-final languages such as Japanese, Korean, telugu, Tamil, Kannada, Bengali, Assamese, Hindi-Urdu, Kashmiri, Mizo, Hmar, Angami, Rabha, Ao etc. Ho language does not also have any comparative and superlative markers comparable to the *–er* and *–est* of English. Consider the following examples:

(33) pro$_{i}$ baamai -te$^{?}$ -ñ̃$_{i}$ jiliŋ- a
I Bamai than 1sg tall dec
'I am taller than Bamai. '

(34) siita$_{i}$ somi -te$^{?}$ -i$_{i}$ ceehra- ge- ^{y}a
Sita Somi than 3sg beautiful emph dec
'Sita is more beautiful than Somi. '

(35) siita isu pura ceehra- ge- ^{y}a
Sita very much beautiful emph dec
'Sita is very much beautiful. '

In Angami, the comparative marker that occurs with the standard of comparison in (36) is *ki* 'than' and the comparison marker that occurs with the adjective is *kO.*

Angami (Tibeo-Burman)
(36) abumO –e tsibu ki puo cha rIkrie kO
Abuno-NOM Tsibu than 3sg height tall comparison marker
'Abuno is taller than Tsibu.'

Subbarao observed that in some Tibeto-Burman languages there are markers which he labelled as Adjectival Comparison Markers(ACM) occur, Thue, these markers are similar to the markers *–er* and *–est* in English. However, the ACM may not be present in Ho like languages such as Telugu, Tamil, Hindi, Bengali, Oriya etc.

Assamese (Indo-Aryan)
(37) xita gitat -koi dhunia Ø

Sita Gita than beautiful ACM
'Sita is more beautiful than Gita.'

In Santali, comparison is expressed by the ablative case, which is attached to the standard of comparison. There are some intensifiers, which can be added for clarification: *b'ti* 'more' and *ar, arho* 'more'.

And degrees of comparison are not expressed in So:ra as in English. Thus, literally the sentence as like 'You are big, I am small' is used. Such words as *boi-boi, aggada* 'very' or 'much' are prefixed to adjectives to express a higher degree.

8. Time and place adverbial

Like in other verb-final languages, in Ho too, time adverbials (T) precede place adverbials (P) as well as P precedes T in unmarked sentence.

(38)	pro $_i$	jaacuila	-re-	^{y}o-	jaata$^{?}$a-	re-	^{y}o-	ñ̃ $_i$	jagar	-dai	$^{-y}$a
	I	*anytme*	*in*	*emph*	*anywhere*	*in*	*emph*	*I sg*	*talk*	*can*	*dec*

'I can talk anytime anywhere. '

(39)	pro $_i$	jaata$^{?}$a	-re-	^{y}o	jaacuila-	re-	^{y}o-	ñ̃ $_i$	jagar	-dai	$^{-y}$a
	I	*anywhere*	*in*	*Emph*	*anytime*	*in*	*emph*	*I sg*	*talk*	*can*	*dec*

'I can talk anytime anywhere. '

A) Order of time and place adverbials

Time and place adverbials occur in descending order. By descending order we mean the bigger chunk of place or time occurs first, then it is followed by a smaller chunk and then a much smaller chunk (Subbarao 1984).

And adverbials of time and place in Ho are posited after the subject in unmarked sentences, but when the subject and object are pronouns and they get dropped then the adverbial can be posited preverbal position.

Let us examine the following sentences.

(40)	añ̃	-a	baba $_i$	hola	pro $_j$	poisa	-e $_i$	em	-aD	-iñ $_i$	^{y}a
	I	*gen*	*Father*	*yesterday*	*me*	*money*	*IIIsg*	*give*	*Pst.pef*	*I sg*	*dec*

'My father had given money to me yesterday. '

(41)	pro $_i$	pro $_j$	iskul	-re	ñ̃ $_i$	nel	-aD	-mi $_j$	$^{-y}$a
	I	*you*	*school*	*in*	*I sg*	*see*	*pst.pef*	*IIsg*	*dec*

'I had seen you in the school. '

(42)	pro$_i$	gapa	bar	baje-ñ$_i$	seno	-^{w}a
	I	*tomorrow*	*two*	*Time*	*go*	*dec*

'I will go at 2 o'clock tomorrow.'

(43)	pro$_i$	caibasa	-re	Johar	-re	-ñ$_i$	paiti	-tan	-a
	I	*Chaibasa*	*in*	*Johar*	*in*	*1sg*	*work*	*pres*	*dec*

'I work in Johar in Chaibasa.'

Rabha (Tibeto-Burman)

(44) cing	asam	hasong	-i	guwahati	-ni	miujiam	ci –na	reng	-ata	-mUn
we	*Assam*	*state*	*of*	*Guwahati*	*of*	*museum*	*see to*	*go*	*PST*	*PERF*

'We had gone to see the museum of Guwahati of Assam State.'

B) Adverbial clause

Before we see adverbial clauses, let us also consider adverbs in Ho. Some roots which usually serve as nouns, adjectives, or verbs can serve as adverbs by adding *–te* 'by' or *–lekate* 'like' to the root as followings (Burrows:1980) :

(45.a)	kurkur -te	(45.b)	bugi -te	(45.c)	bugi -lekate
	angry -by		*good –by*		*good -by*
	'angrily'		'well'		'well'

(46.a)	ne -lekate	(46.b)	okon -lekate	(46.c)	hola –lekate
	this –like		*what -like*		*yesterday –like*
	'in this way'		'in what manner'		'like it was yesterday'

By definition adverbials are that grammatical category which modifies verbs adjectives, other adverbs, phrases or sentences. The notions range of adverbs varies with the type of constituent modified. For example, the adverb which modifies verbs or verb phrases usually express time, place, direction manner, etc. and those which modify adjectives and adverbs commonly express degree. Here, wewill see only four types of adverbial clauses of Ho. They are adverbial clauses of Reason, adverbial clauses of Manner, adverbial clauses of Purpose and adverbial clauses of time.

C) Adverbial Clauses of Time

The main type of constructions used to express a temporal relationship between the action of a subordinate clause and the action of its associated main clause are as follows:

(47)	*am*	*seno-*	*tan*	*taiomte*	*añ-yo*	*seno-*	*tan-*	*a*
	you	go	pres	after	I -emph	go	prog	dec

'After you go, I am also going'.

D) Adverbial Clauses of Location

Adverbial clauses of location in Ho are introduced by the subordinators such as *okonre*, *okonte*, *okonpare*. All these are three different forms of the English word – 'where'. Out of these three forms *okonre* signify anywhere, akonpare signify specific place and *okonte* signify the normal where. And we can also used subordinator like *taiomte* – 'after' to form adverbial clauses of location in Ho.

(48) okonte am$_i$ seno -len -a -m$_i$ (añ$_j$) seno- tan- a -ñ$_j$

Where you go pst dec you I go prog –dec -I

'Where you have gone I am going.'

E) Adverbial clauses of Purpose

Adverbial clauses of purpose in Ho is introduced by using the subordinator such as redo – 'if', re – 'by', etc. Let us see some examples by using the above subordinators.

(49)	lija	-ko	tapai-	tan-	re	jan	lab	bano	-a
	cloth	*pl*	*wash*	*prog*	*by*	*any*	*gain*	*nothing*	*dec*

'No gain by washing clothes.

The above example (49) might shows that the declartive marker *–a* cannot not occur in the matrix clause.

(50)	añ	nenta$^{?}$a	-re	men-	yan-	te	bar	sirme	hoba	yan	-a
	I	*here*	*at*	*stay*	*pst*	*since*	*two*	*year*	*happen*	*pst*	*dec*

'It has been two years since I have been here'.

(51)	ne-pe-l-	-redo	(-laŋ)	alaŋ$_{i}$	ki-pi-ring-	a-	laŋ$_{i}$
	see-reciprocal	*if*	*-dual*	*we(dual)*	*trade-reciprocal*	*dec*	*-1dual*

'If we see each other, we will trade together'.

F) Adverbial Clauses of Reason

Adverbial clauses f reason is similar to purpose adverbial clauses in the sense that is most commonly expressed the motivating event which may be realized at the time of the main clause event, while the purpose classes express the motivating event which must be unrealized at the time of event.

(52)	owa$^{?}$	seno	-re	enga	lo$^{?w}$a	be-pe-ta	hoba-	yan-	a
	home	*go*	*by*	*mother*	*with*	*meet*	*happen*	*pst*	*dec*

'By going home you met your mother'.

9. Complementation

Complementation is a [henomenon in which the main clause and the subordinate clause are linked by a linking device. As in the sentence '*We knew that we would win the race'*, *that* links the main clause and the subordinate clause and the verb *know* permints the subordinate clause to occur as its complement and the linker is called a complimentizer.

The complementizer which is a form of verb *say* follows the subordinate clause as in Mizo, Hmar and Manipuri of the Tibeto-Burman language family, Assamese, Bengali, Oriya, Nepali, Konkani, Marathi of the Indo-Aryan language family and in Telugu, Tamil, Kannada, Malayalam of the Dravidian language family. In Korean and Japanese too thecomplementizer occurs to the right of the subordinate clause.

There is only a pre-sentential (left peripheral) complementizer in Ho.

(53)

añ	kaji-	keD-	a	ci	(am)$_i$	kiteb-	ko-	m $_i$	kiriŋ-	keD-	a
I	*say*	*pst*	*dec*	*comp*	*you*	*book*	*pl*	*IIsg*	*buy*	*pst*	*Dec*

'I told that you bought books. '

(54)

soma	kaji-	keD-	a	ci	(añ)$_i$	dilli-	iñ $_i$	seno-	tan-	a
Soma	*say*	*pst*	*dec*	*comp*	*I*	*Delhi*	*I sg*	*go*	*prog*	*dec*

'Soma said that I am going to Delhi. '

In (53) and (54) there is no matrix subject agreement in embedded clauses. And in (55) below sentence the second complementizer is optional after the conjunction in embedded clauses.

[5](55) ini$^{?}$ $_i$	adaan –a	– i$_i$	ci	ritu	huju-	len	-a	ondo (ci)	kamla	seno -^{y}en	-a
she	*know*	*dec*	*IIIsg* *comp*	*Ritu*	*come*	*pst*	*dec*	*and*	*comp Kamla*	*go* *pst*	*dec*

'She knows that Ritu came and Kamla left. '

---

[5] But in (55) we find that there is no subject agreement in the embedded clause. Because the matrix subject and embedded subject both are 3rd singular. So it is not necessary to reduplicate 3rd sg Agr.

(56)

am	kaji	-keD	-a	ci	pro$_i$	pro$_j$	poisa	-m$_i$	em	-aD	-iñ$_j$	-a
you	*say*	*pst*	*dec*	*comp*	*you*	*me*	*money*	*IIsg*	*give*	*pst*	*I sg*	*dec*

'You said that you gave me money. '

In (56) we can see that the matrix subject cannot be dropped while the embedded subject can be dropped if the matrix and embedded subject is identical.

Let us look at more examples.

(57) am$_i$	añ$_j$	poisa	-m$_i$	ema	iñ$_j$	-a	ci	am	kaji	ke-D	-a
you	*I*	*money*	*2sg*	*give*	*1sg*	*dec*	*comp*	*2s.g.*	*say*	*pst*	*dec*

'You told me that you will give me money.'

(58) inka	atakaro-wa	ci	soma	owa?	seno	ye	n	-a
this	*possible-dec*	*comp*	*pro*	*house*	*go*	*pres*	*[-tr]*	*dec*

'It is possible that Soma goes there'

(59) ram	onDo	gopal	cinaa	kaji	keD	a
ram	*and*	*gopal*	*what*	*say*	*pst*	*dec*

'What did Ram and Gopal say?'

(60) soma	cinaa	kaji	taD	a
soma	*what*	*say*	*pres*	*dec*

'What is Soma say?'

(61) inka	aTakarowa	(ci)	gopal	owa?	seno	yen	a
this	*possible*	*comp*	*gopal*	*home*	*go*	*pst*	*dec*

'It is possible that Gopal went home'

(62) Ø	a^{y}e$^?$	dai	akachaka	tan	-a
	he	*win*	*surprise*	*pres*	

'That he won is surprising'

(63) (ci) a^{y}e$^{?}$ dai akachaka tan -a

he win surprise pres dec

'That he won is surprising'

(64) añ$_{i}$ am$_{j}$ geliya kuihon ko -ñ$_{i}$ em aD im$_{j}$ ya

I you ten girl pl 1s.g give pst 2s.g. dec

'I gave you ten girls.'

(65) (ci) a^{y}e dilii seno tan -a

comp she delhi go pres dec

'That she will go to Delhi'

(66) ako na ajoŋ epa ka ko huju$^{?}$ len -a

they yet here not pl come pst dec

'They did not come here yet'

(67)ram ka -e$^{?}$ uRu-^{w}e ci a^{y}e jaai-ri -a aDaan -a

Ram not 3s.g. Think comp he anybody know dec

'Ram doesn't think that he knows anybody.'

10. Adjectives

The adjective precedes the head noun. And in Ho the adjective does not exhibits the agreement in number and person and gender.

(68) ini$^{?}$ -ta$^{?}$a isu maraŋ owa$^{?}$ min -a
he near very big house is dec
'He has a very big house. '

The adjective occurs with the verb 'be' or the declarative marker. But the verb 'be' and the declarative marker are optional in the present tense while it is obligatory in the past tense.

(69) en sepeD bugin - min -a = en sepeD bugin -ø –a = en sepeD bugin –ø -ø
that boy good is dec
'That boy is good. '

(70) en sepeD bugin *(tai ken –a)
that boy good was dec
'That boy was good. '

And in Ho some adjectives and nouns have same form.

(71) a^{y}e$^{?}$ reŋge -tan -a
he hungry is
'He is hungry. '

(72) a^{y}e -$^{?}$a reŋge maraŋ -a
he gen hunger big dec
'His hunger is big. '

(73) añ hasu -min -a
I painful is dec
'I am painful. '

(74) añ -a hasu min- a
I gen pain is dec
'I have pain. '

In above examples, *rabaŋ* 'cold, coldness' is also an adjective as well as a noun.

Note that the adjective in Rabha behaves like a verb like in many Tibeto-Burman languages. In Rabha, the adjectivalizer *–kay* occurs when the adjective modifies a noun. However, when the adjective occurs in the predicate position *–kay*, the adjectivailzer, cannot occur. Instead, the tense marker occurs. And *–kay* occurs as a gerundival marker too.

Rabha (Tibeto-Burman)

(75)	park	-i	-na	reng	kay	nem	-a
	park	*LOC*	*DAT*	*go*	*-ing*	*good*	*pres*

'Going to a park is good.'

(76)	ak	-kay	to	kuli	(be)	si	-jO
	black	*ADJR*	*fowl*	*female*	*NOM*	*die*	*res.perf.*

'The black female fowl is dead.'

(77)	masunu	nem	-a
	cow milk	*good*	*PRES*

'Cow milk is good.'

In So:ra, the words derived from such adjectives preserves the distinction of gender unlike Ho. As we already observed, in Ho, adjectives are invariable: they are notaffected by the gender of number of the noun they qualify. Most Ho adjectives may without any change of form be used as nouns or verbs, or, to put the matter in its correct sequence, the original root can be used as a verb, noun or adjective without the addition of any secondary root to denote that its meaning has been altered. However, adjectives do undergo achange of form sometimes, though such cases must be regarded as exceptional. Thus the suffixes *–n* and *–an* are added to a few verbs and nouns to for adjectives as shown in followings:

(78a) etka 'to be bad' → etkan 'bad'

(78b) bisi 'poison' → bisian 'poisonous'

(78c) pe 'strength' → pean 'strong'

The adjective does not exhibit agreement with the modifying noun in Rabha like in Manipuri. This is expected because verbs in Rabha too do not carry any agreement marker. There are two types of adjectives: (1) verbal adjectives and (2) deverbal adjectives.

11. Determiners and articles

While some Tibeto-Burman languages have a split determiner system where the determiner precedes and follows the noun phrase, in Ho language the determiner only precede the head noun.

(79) en sepeD bugin -min -a
that boy good is dec
'That boy is good. '

(80) owa? - re
house in
'In the house'

There is no indication of any sort of the definite article in (79) and (80). Rabha also does not exhibit a split determiner system though some Tibeto-Burman languages such as Mizo, Hmar have a split determiner system. However, determiners exhibit number agreement in Rabha. Both the determiner and the noun carry plural marker when the nou is [+human]. But the plural marker –tang may be optionally dropped. For examplefrom Rabha:

(81a) o –kay kay
that ADJR man
'That man'

(81b) o -bizan kay -tang
that PL man PL
'Those men'

(81c) o -bizan kay -ø
that PL man -PL
'Those men'

In Ho the plural marker can occur once to the right of the noun. And it does not seeem to have the classifier. Thus, the determiner and adjective precede the noun but the classifer does not follow the noun

12. Numerals

Ho numbers form 1 to 10 have a long and a short form.

number	long form	short form	number	long form	short form
1	mi^{y}ed'	mid'	6	turui^{y}a	turui
2	bari^{y}a	bar	7	ai^{y}a	ai
3	api^{y}a	ape	8	irle^{y}a	iril
4	upuni^{y}a	upun	9	are^{y}a	are
5	mo^{y}a	moe	10	gele^{y}a	gel
11	gel mi^{y}ed'		20	hisi	
30	hisi gele^{y}a / dosi		40	bar hisi	

According to Lionel Burrows, the numbers from 1 to 10 inclusive, and 20, have separate forms. Between 10 and 20, the numbers are formed by adding the first nine numbers to the shortened form for 10. The numbers above 20 are calculated in stages of twenties. After ten the cardinal numbers are as follows:

11: gel-mi$_y$ed' (ten and one)

12:gel-bari$_y$a (ten an two)

24: hisi-upunia$_y$a (twenty and four)

As seen in the table above, the number 30 is the form of 'twenty + ten'. However, the separate form for the number 30 can be also used: *dosi*(Deeney 1966). And the number 40 and 60 can be interpretated as 'two times twenty' and 'three times twenty', respectively. When the short form of any compound number is required the short form of the final number is used, i.e. 13: gel-api$_y$a / gel-ape.

Ho has no proper terms for ordinal numbers. Thus ordinal numbers have to be expressed by some round about way. except fiirst : *sida* or *ayera* and second : *eta*$^?$·

For the higher numbers the following constructions are use, and the sense is generally made clearer by pointing out the object where possible (Burrows 1980).

(82a) upun ho-ko taiomre-ni agu-i-me

four people-pl after -participle bring-3sg-imperative

'Bring the fifth man.'

(82b) upun ho-ko bage-ked -ko-te miyad agu –i –me

four people-pl leave-pst –3pl-by one bring-3sg-imperative

'Bring the fifth man.'

To make an adjective of a cardinal number, the vowel occurring finally with these numbers is generally and that occurring medially is sometimes dropped.

Santali cardinal numerals from one to ten and the ordinals from fourth to tenth have cognates in other Munda languages, higher numbers are composed and or borrowed (Neukom: 1998). In Santali when a numeral is used as an attributed to a noun, a classifer is often suffixed to it. The classifiers do not occur without preceding numerals. There are two types of classifers: one is for human beings and the other is for the general. Moerover, the numeral *mit* 'one' + classifer is used as indefinite article: it introduces a new referent which is relevant for the subsequent discourse.

In So:ra: no ordinal numbers and classifiers exhibit. And the So:ra: counts up to twelve. Tthe following numbers up to twenty are formed by adding the first seven numerals to twelve.

13. Relative clauses

In Ho there is a fully-fledged strategy as well as a gap strategy for relative clauses, namely they use either relative pronouns or participle so as in Hindi and So:ra:. And it is, of course, a Head External Relative Clause. Let us consider the following examples:

(1)

en sepeD$_i$ okun$_i$ puti -e$_i$ paRaaw -tan -a pro$_i$ murkuu -e

that boy who book sg read Prog dec stupid dec+3sg

'That boy who is reading a book is stupid. '

(2)

en sepedD$_i$ murkuu -e okun$_i$ kiteb -i$_i$ paRaaw -tan -a

that boy stupid Dec+3sg who book 3sg read prog

'That boy is stupid who is reading a book. '

(3)

okun$_i$ sepeD$_i$ puti -e$_i$ paRaaw -tan -a ro murkuu -e

who boy book 3sg read prog dec stupid dec+3sg

'That boy is stupid who is reading a book '

In sentences (1) to (3), the relative clause has three types of the word order as followed in:

a) NP + S_2 + VP

b) NP + VP + S_2

c) S_2 + NP + VP

(4a)

en kuihon$_i$ okoni$_i$ jaho añ -a owa$^?$ -e$_i$ huju -e(ini)$_I$ añ-a juri

that girl who everyday emph I gen house 3sg come dec this I genfriend

'The girl who comes to my house everyday is my friend.'

(4b)

en kuihon -ko$_i$ okonko$_i$ jaho -ge añ -a owa$^{?}$ -ko$_i$ huju -e (ini)$_i$ añ -a juRi-ko

that girl pl who everyday emph I gen house 3sg come dec this I gen friend-3pl

'The girls who come to my house everyday is my friend.'

(5a) en topi $_i$ okona $_i$ tebul -re min -a (ena) $_i$ bugin -a

that hat which table on is dec that nice dec

'That hat which is on the table is nice.'

(5b) en topi -ko $_i$ okonako $_i$ tebul -re min -a (enako) $_i$ bugin -a

that hat pl which table on is dec that nice dec

'That hats which are on the table are nice.'

The sentences (4) and (5) indicate that the subject agreement marker also occurs to the relative pronoun.

(6)

en ku^{w}ahon $_i$ okoni $_i$ puti $_j$ -e $_i$ paraaw -e $_j$ -tan -a (ini) $_i$ cuutur -gi -^{y}a

that boy who book 3sg read 3sg prog dec this intelligent emph dec

'The boy who is reading a book is intelligent.'

Actually, however, it is not really true that we can apply the above word order to all different types of relative pronouns. e.g.in cases of OO, GEN and O COMP. And if we test Keenan and Comrie's (1977, 1979) Noun Phrase Accessibility Hierarchy (NAPH), there is no skip position in Ho.

SUB > DO > IO > OO > GEN > O COMP

The relative clause can modify subject, direct object, indirect object, oblique object and object of the genitive. By oblique object we mean the object of instrumental, ablative, locative and comitative positions. It is generally agreed that if a noun phrase at the lower end of the hierarchy can be relativized, all noun phrases above that position can be relativized without any exception. However, in some languages there might be some exceptions.

Direct Object:

The entire embedded relative clause modifies the object. However the embedded relative clause does not occur to the left of the head noun without the help of the participle in Ho.

(7a)
en samosa $_i$ okona ñ̃ -a juRi jom -leD a pro $_i$ $^{e?}$ka -a
that samosa which y gen friend eat pst.pef dec useless dec
'That Samosa which my friend had eaten was useless. '

(7b)
en samosa -ko $_i$ okonako $_i$ añ-a juri jom -led-a (enako) $_I$ ek$^?$ataiken a
Tha tsamosa pl which Igen friend eat pst pf dec those useless were dec
'The samosas which my friend had eaten were useless.'

(8)
en samosa -ko $_i$ ek$^?$a taiken -a okonako $_i$ añ -a Ri om
that samosa pl useless were dec which I gen friend at
'The samosas which my friend had eaten were useless.'

(9) okon $_i$ samosa -ko $_i$ añ -a juri jom -leD -a (enako) $_i$ ek$^?$a taiken -a
which samosa pl I gen friend eat pst pf dec those useless were dec
'The samosas which my friend had eaten were useless.'

(10)
en sita $_i$ okoni $_i$ añ sukut -i $_i$ - ^{y}e (ini) $_i$ hola añ -a owa$^?$ huju -len -a
that dog which I like 3sg de this yesterday I gen house come pst pf dec
'The dog which I like had come to my house yesterday.'

Indirect Object

The embedded relative clause midifying the indirect object occurs to the right of the head noun without the postpotion or the dative case marker.

(11)

en ho$_i$ okoe$_i$ pro$_j$ ciTTi -m$_j$ ool -leD -i$_i$ -^{y}a salaŋ -e

that person whom you letter 2sg write pst.pef 3sg dec tall dec+3sg

'That person whom you had written a letter is tall. '

(12)

okon$_i$ bilai$_i$ añ haku$_j$ em-aD-i$_j$-e (ini)$_i$ esu bugin-tai ken-a

which cat I fish give pst 3sg dec this very cute be pst dec

'The cat to which I gave a fish was cute.'

By oblique object we mean a noun phrase in the oblique case. The oblique case includes ablative as in '**from** the well', instrumental as in '**with** a knife', locative as in '**on** the table', or comitative as in '**with** my friends'. The postposition in bold from, with, on are oblique case markers.

Locative

The head noun which is case-marked by the postpositon occurs inside the relative clause.

(13)

pro$_i$ okon$_j$ tebul$_j$ -re manDi -m$_i$ em -ekaD -a maraŋ -a

you which table on food 2sg give pres.pef dec big dec

' The table on which you have kept the food is big. '

(14)

en tebul$_i$ okon$_i$ -re pro$_j$ manDi -m$_j$ em -a keD -a (ena)$_i$ maraŋ -a

that table which on you food 2sg put epen pst dec that big dec

'The table on which you put the food is big.'

(15)

okon$_i$ gaRi -re am dub -tan -a en gaRi$_i$ ini-^{y}a

which car in you sit prog dec that car hers

'The car in which you are sitting is hers.'

(16)

en gaRi$_i$ okon$_i$-re añ dub -tan -a (ena)$_i$ ini^y

that car which in I sit prog dec that hers

'The car in which I am sitting is hers.'

Instrumental

(17)

kon$_i$ cakuu$_i$ -te pro$_j$ uutu -ko$_j$ haaDe tan -a (encakuu) leser -a

whic knife they veg 3pl cut prog dec that knife sharp dec

'The knife with which they are cutting the vegetable is sharp. '

(18)

en kaatuu okona$_i$ -te ako$_j$ utuui -^{y}a ko$_j$ haDe tan -a leser -a

the knife which with they veg epen 3pl cut prog dec that sharp

'The knife which with they are cutting the veg. is sharp.'

(19)

ena en cabi$_i$ -ge okona$_i$ -te añ$_j$ baksh -añ$_j$ nii$^?$ -keD -a

that the key emph which with I box Isg open pst dec

'That is the key with which I opened the box.'

Ablative

(20)

okon$_i$ pro$_j$ bajar$_i$ (-re) -te uutu -ko$_j$ kiriŋ -keD -a , sapa -gi -^{y}a

whic they market in from veg 3pl buy pst dec clean emph dec

'The market from which they bought the vegetable is clean. '

(21)

okon$_i$ hua$_i$ ete pro$_j$ daa$^?$ ñ$_j$ idi keD -a (ena) ikiR-giya

which well from I water 1sg fetch pst dec that deep

'The well from which I fetched the water is deep.'

(22)

en taiaD$_i$ aben$_j$ okonta$_i$ -ete -ben$_j$ huju -tan -a (ena)$_i$ esu-ssaniŋ-a

that place you(dl) which from 2pl come prog dec that veryfardec

'The place from which you are coming is very far.'

Commitative

(23)

am okon$_i$ ku^{w}atan ko lo$^?$o$_i$ huju -^{w}akan -a (enko) esu -ko salaŋ -a

2 whom boy pl with come pres.pef dec they very 3pl tall dec

'The boys with whom you have came are very tall. '

(24)

en ku^{w}ahon$_i$ okoni$_i$ am -loo$^?$ -e$_i$ huju -len -a (ini)$_i$ jiliŋ -a

the boy who you with 3sg come pstpf dec this tall dec

'The boy with whom you had come is tall.'

en$_i$ okoni$_i$ am loo$^?$ e$_i$ huju len esu burbek -gi -^{y}a

the dog which you with 3sg come pstpf dec that very stupid emph dec

'The dog with whom you had come is very stupid.'

Object of Genitive

(26) pro$_i$ en -hon$_j$ -ñ$_i$ sanaŋ -ti^{y}e okuni -^{y}a$_j$ enga bugin -a

I that man Isg like for whose gen mother nice dec

'I like that man whose mother is nice. '

(27)

en bilai$_i$ okoni^{y}a$_i$ chadlom haDe -i -ken -a (ini)$_i$ husiyar -giya

the cat whose tail cut epen pst dec this intelligent emph dec

'The cat whose tail was cut is intelligent.'

Object of Comparison

(28)

en	-kui tan	-i $_i$	okoni $_i$	$a^{y}e$	-te	salaŋ	-a	añ	-a	misikui	-tan	-a
that	*girl*	*3sg*	*who*	*him*	*than*	*tall*	*dec*	*I*	*gen*	*sister*	*is*	*dec*

' That girl who is taller than him is my sister. '

(29)

en	huriŋ	seta $_i$	okon $_i$	-ete	en	maraŋ	bilai $_j$	landi	-i $_j$	$-^{y}e$	giti	-tan	-a
that	*small*	*dog*	*who*	*than*	*the*	*big*	*cat*	*lazy*	*3sg*	*dec*	*sleep*	*prog*	*dec*

'The small dog than whom the big cat is lazier is sleeping.'

Let us now examine the Post-EHRC in Ho which is verb-final language. The form of the presenting NP_{RC} is the participle[6] as the use of gapping strategies. Ho also has relative relative clause in which the head noun of the embedded relative clause is not overtly present.

Such types of clauses are the result f the gap strategy. In the gap strategy the relative clause occurs pronominally, i.e. to the left of the head noun. In the gap strategy the embedded verb is always in the non-finite form (without a tense marker) like in most of the Tibeto-Burman languages.

The non-finite form of the embedded verb in many Tibeto-Burman languages is a participial form of the verb. However, in the gap stategy the embedded verb is always in the Finite form (with a tense marker).

Thus, there is no participial form for the gap stategy. But there is of course a conjunctive participle with the tense marker in Ho. Let us consider the following examples:

(30) [	hola	seno	$-^{y}an$	]	ho	apu	-ñ
	yesterday	*come*	*pst*		*man*	*father*	*I sg=gen*

---

[6] In Ho participles are formed simply by dropping the declarative marker *–a* from the VP, regardless of its tense etc.

‘ The man who came yesterday is my father. ’

[Gap$_i$ + VP_1 + null-participle] Head NP$_i$ VP_2

Participial Relative Clause

(31)	[a^{y}e$^?$	sabii	-ø]	kula$_i$	añ	-ta$^?$a	–re	agu	–i$_i$	-pe
	he	*catch*	*fut*	*tiger*	*me*	*near*	*to*	*bring*	*3sg*	*imp*

‘Bring to me the tiger which you will catch ’

In Ho forming a participial relative clause is that only declarative marker *–a* is dropped. But the declative marker *–a* is oftenly present in normal speech.

(32)	en	ku^{w}ahon	-ko	huju	-tan	-a
	that	*boy*	*pl*	*come*	*prog*	*dec*

‘The boys are coming.’

(33)	añ	-a	owa$^?$	huju	-tan	ku^{w}ahon	-ko$_i$	añ	-a	juRi	-ko$_i$
	I	*gen*	*house*	*come*	*prog*	*boy*	*pl*	*I*	*gen*	*friend*	*pl*

‘The boys who are coming to my house are my friends.’

The above sentences show that the declartive marker is dropped in the gap strategy. However in the following sentence, the declartive marker occurs the left of the head noun. Actually it is not clear whether it is the case of scrambling or not.

(34)	pro$_i$	haku	-m$_i$	kiriŋ	-leD	-a
	you	*fish*	*2sg*	*buy*	*pstpf*	*dec*

‘You had bought a fish.’

(35)	am	kiriŋ	-leD	-a	haku	maraŋ	-tai	-ken	-a
	you	*buy*	*pstpf*	*dec*	*fish*	*big*	*be*	*pst*	*dec*

‘The fish you had bought was big.’

(36)	hora	-re	seno	-tan	ku^{w}ahon$_i$	kiya	-i$_i$	me
	road	*on*	*walk*	*pres,prog*	*boy*	*call*	*3sg*	*imp 2sg*

‘Call the boy who is walking on the road.’

(37) okon$_i$ ho$_i$ hora -re seno -tan -a ini$_i$ kiya -i -me

which man road on walk prog dec he call 3sg imp2sg

'Call the man who is walking on the road.'

(38) pro$_i$ hora$_j$ -re seno -tan ho kiya -i$_j$ -me$_i$

you road on walk prog man call 3sg imp2sg

'Call the man who is walking on the road.'

Free Relatives

In English free relatives have the relative pronouns whoever, whatever, whomever, whenever etc. Free relatives normally occur as full-fledged relatives with an over relative pronoun. They do not permit the Gap strategy. There is dubitative marker –*ina* in Ho, but it is not obligatory. And the form of free relatives is not similar to relative pronouns and interrogative words. It is illustrated in the following examples:

(39) jai$_i$ –re –^{y}o johar ofis -re huju -a -(ina), (añ) sukut -i$^?{}_i$ -^{y}eñ

anyone emph Johar office to come dec dubi I like 3sg dec + Isg

'Whoever comes to Johar office, I like. '

(40) jaai$_i$ -ge ayerte huju -^{w}a ini$_i$ -ge baksis$_j$ nam -i$_j$ -^{y}a

whoever emph first come dec he emph prize get 3sg dec

'Whoever comes firs, he will get the prize.'

(41) pro$_i$ jai$_j$ -m$_i$ sukut -i$_j$ –^{y}e –(ini), añ$_x$ -^{y}o -ñ$_x$ sukut –i$_j$ -^{y}e

you anyone 2sg like 3sg dec dubi I emph I sg like IIIsg dec

'Whomever you like, I also like. '

(42) pro$_i$ jana$_j$ -m$_i$ jom -e$_j$ -^{y}a –(ina) añ$_x$ - ^{y}o -ñ$_x$ jom -e$_j$ -^{y}a

you anything 2sg eat 3sg dec dubi I emph I sg eat IIIsg dec

'Whatever you eat, I also eat. '

(43) hon –ko$_i$ jana$_j$ -ko$_i$ jom -e$_j$ -^{y}a –(ina) añ$_x$ - ^{y}o -ñ$_x$ jom -e$_j$ -^{y}a

children anything 3pl eat 3sg dec dubi I emph I sg eat IIIsg dec

'Whatever children eat, I also eat.'

(44) pro $_i$ jaacimi -te -m $_i$ seno -a -(imitan) añ -^{y}o -ñ seno -a
you anytime 2sg go dec dubi I emph I sg go dec
'Whenever you go, I also go.'

(45) pro $_i$ jaatam -te -m $_i$ seno -a -(ina) añ -^{y}o -ñ seno -a
you anywhere 2sg go dec dubi I emph I sg go dec
'Wherever you go, I also go.'

According to Ramamurti (1931), in So:ra: there are also two kinds of clauses. One is introduced by the conjunctive particle -*ə* and end in in *–(ə)n* followed by *ə*-, and the othere is introduced by the relative pronouns. Finite verbs are of course used along with their objects and other and other adjuncts, if required.

14. Negative

In Ho, there seems to be no morphological negation. But as for the preverbal negation, it is represented by the morpheme [*ka-*] which must come immediately before the verb. The subject agreement marker must be suffixed to the negative. The negative *ka-* cannot occur alone without the subject agreement marker except in some cases[7].

Forms of Negation:

(a)	*ka*	(no)
(b)	*ka .... ka*	(neither .... nor)
(c)	*alom*	(Imperative)
(d)	*ka – agr*	(without)

The negative form ka corresponds to either the pro-sentence no in English sentence like. 'No, I am not happy' or not in English which is used for sentential negation along with ka-agrs. The following examples illustrate the case in Ho.

(46)	ka	aye$^{?}_{i}$	ka-$^{?}$e$_{i}$	bugin	a
	neg	*he*	*neg-3sg*	*well*	*dec*

'No, she is not well'.

(47)	ka	gama	ka – $^{?}$e	iyu$^{?}$u	tan	a
	neg	*rain*	*Neg-3sg*	*rain*	*prs.prog*	*dec*

'No, it is not raining'.

(48)	ini$^{?}$	ka	- $^{?}$e	bugin	a
	3.sg	*neg -*	*3sg*	*happy*	*dec*

'She is not happy'.

(49)	aye$^{?}$	owa$^{?}$-re	ka –$^{?}$e	baŋga	i ye
	3.sg	*room.pp*	*neg-*	*exist*	*dec*

'She is not in the room'.

---

[7] We will see some exceptional cases in relation with the agreement section.

(50) pro $_i$ gapa en -ta$^{?}$a ka *(-$^{?}$e)$_i$ seno ø -a

he tomorrow that near not 3sg go fut dec

'He will not go tomorrow. '

(51) pro $_i$ musiŋ -musiŋ ka -ko $_i$ unuŋ -tan -a

they often often not 3pl play pres dec

'Not often they play. '

(52) ka , gama $_i$ ka -$^{?}$e $_i$ i^{y}u$^{?}$u -tan -a

no , rain not 3sg fall prog dec

'No, it is not raining. '

In (52) *ka-* itself means 'no' as well as 'not'. And there is no [+animate] subject. But the subject agreement occurred to the right of the negation. It seems to be due to this that the natural phenomenon is regarded as [+animate] in Ho.

(53) ciken re^{y}a ka -$^{?}$a -ge ?

why emph not dec emph ?

'Why not ? '

(54) a^{y}e$^{?}$ uRu -tan -a ci [pro$_i$ jaai -re-^{y}o ka -$^{?}$e $_i$ aDaan -a]

he think pres dec comp anyone emph not 3sg know dec

'He thinks that he does not know anyone. '

(55) a^{y}e$^{?}$ ka -$^{?}$e $_i$ uRu -tan -a ci [pro$_i$ jaai -re-^{y}o aDaan-a

he not 3sg think pres dec comp anyone emph know

'He does not think that he knows anyone. '

ka ... ka (Neither – nor)

(56) aye$^{?}$ ka-$^{?}$e rããsa – ^{w}a ondo$^{?}$ ka – $^{?}$e – ge bugin – a

he neg-3sg sad – dec and neg–3sg- emph happy-.dec

'She is neither sad nor happy'.

(57) aye$^{?}$ ka – $^{?}$e unuŋ-tan-a ondo$^{?}$ ka – $^{?}$e paraw tan – a

he neg-3sg play –pres-dec and neg-agrs study prog- dec

'She is neither playing nor studying'.

(58) añ nenta?a – re am – a denga – te ka - ñ tain dai - a

I here-in your help. with neg.agrs stay can. dec

'I can't stay here without your help'.

The affirmative form of the above sentence

(59) añ nenta?a – re am – a denga – te-ñ tain dai - a

I here-in- your help-by-1sg stay can. dec

'I can stay here with your help'.

Negative interrogative construction

(60) aye$^{?}$ ka –$^{?}$ e duraŋ dai – a ci

he neg-3sg sing can-dec Q.mkr

'Can't she sing?'

Negative and Affirmative answer

(61) añ - a juri$_{i}$ huju tan – a-^{w}e$_{i}$ ci

my friend come pres-dec-3sg Q.mkr.

'Is my friend coming?'

(62) iya añ - a juri huju tan – a-we

yes my friend come pres- dec-3sg

'Yes, my friend has come'.

(63) ka añ - a juri$_{i}$ ka –$^{?}$ e$_{i}$ huju tan – a

no my friend neg-3sg come pres- dec

'No, my friend hasn't come.

Negation in Embedded Clause

Payne contends that in the negation of the main and the sub-ordinate clauses, the same negative strategy is not used. For English, Payne says that the position of the negative particle not is pre-verbal in infinitival or genitival clauses, as opposed to post-verbal not in main clauses.

(i) He [is] not poor (post-verbal)

(ii) He expects not [to be] late (pre-verbal)

The negation strategy of negation in HO, however, does not adhere to Payne's statements. In this language there is no dichotomy between the forms involved in negating propositions either in the main or in the embedded / subordinate clauses. The negative particle *ka* is used for negating in both the types of clauses. The following examples will illustrate the point.

Negation of object modifying relative clasue.

(64) en samosa esu jillu- a okon aña judi ka-ˀe jom keD -a

that samosa very bad- dec which my friend neg-3sg eat –pst-dec

'That samosa which my friend hadn't eaten was bad'.

(65) en ho okoe am nikul ka – am ol-led-am (ini) esu jilliŋ -a

that man whom yu letter neg.agr write.pst he very-tall -dec

'That man to whom you didn't write the letter is very tall'.

Negation of Complement clause

(66) añ aye murkur ka - ñ uRu tan – a

I him fool neg-1sg consider prs dec

'I don't consider him to be a fool'.

Adverbial clause

(67) (am)	ka-m	paiti	redo – m	paisa$_{i}$	ka – m	nam – i$^{y}{}_{i}$	a
you	*neg-2sg*	*work*	*if (conj) –2sg*	*money*	*neg-2sg*	*get-3sg*	*dec*

'From not working you don't get money'.

Object complement clause

(68)	a^{y}e$^{?}$	ka –$^{?}$ e	paRaw -lageD	mone	-keD -a
	he	*neg-3sgs*	*study -for*	*decide*	*-pst-dec*

'He decided not to study'.

Question Tag

(69)	aye$^{?}$	ho-^{w}e	jagar – a	ci	ka
	she	*Ho –3sg*	*speak.dec*	*Q.mkr*	*neg*

'She speaks Ho, doesn't she?'

Negative Adverb

(70)	ako	musiŋ – musiŋ	ka –ko	unuŋ	tan –a
	they	*often*	*neg-3pl*	*play*	*pres-dec.*

'Not often they play / They don't often play.'

(71)	mindo	ho – ge	ka –$^{?}$ e	huju	yan – a
	one	*person.-emph*	*neg-agr*	*come*	*pst-dec*

'Not even a person came'.

(72)	barye	ho – kin – ge	ka – kin	huju	yan – a
	two	*person –2dual- emph*	*neg-.dual*	*come.*	*pst - dec*

'Not even two person come'

Negative polarity item

Ho has a number of lexical items to express negative olarity. Some of them are mentioned below.

jaa paa	=	anywhere
jaiiyo	=	anybody

(73)	añ	jaapaa – yo	ka - ñ	seno	tan – a
	I	*anywhere.-emph*	*neg.-1sg*	*go*	*prog-dec*

'I am not going anywhere'.

(74)	jaaii-yo	ka – ko	huju –len – a
	anybody-emph	*neg.agrs*	*come-pst-dec*

'Anybody didn't come.'

(75)	añ - a	juRi	ka –ˀ e	huju	tan – a
	my	*friend*	*neg-3sg*	*come*	*pres-dec*

'My friend is not coming.'

(76)	alle	jaw – ge	ka – le	seno – ʷa
	we	*NPI*	*neg.agrs*	*go -dec*

'We will never go out.'

(77)	alle	jaw-ge	seno-a-le
	we	*always-emph*	*go-dec-1pl*

'We always go out.'

The difference between the last two sentences is the negative particle *ka-*. It shows that the in Ho like English negative polarity items need negative in the sentence to be C-commanded by it. Here *ka* C-commands the NPI never.

Ambiguity

(78)	ayeˀ	uRu – tan – a	ci	ayeˀ	jaana	ka-ˀe	adaan-a
	he	*think-pres-dec*	*that*	*he*	*anything*	*neg –3sg*	*know-dec.*

'He thinks that he doesn't know anything.'

(79)	ayeˀ	ka –ˀ e	uRu – tan – a	ci	ayeˀ	sabin-ho-ko	adaan – a
	he	*neg-3sg*	*think-pres-dec*	*comp*	*he*	*everybody*	*know-dec*

'He dose not think that he knows everybody'.

(80) añ uRu – tan – a ci ka-ˀe gama – ʸa

I think-pres-dec comp neg-3sg rain-dec

'I think (that) it is not raining'.

(81) añ ka - ñ uRu – tan – a ci gama – keD - a

I neg –1sg think-pres-dec comp rain –pst -dec

'I don't think it rained'.

'To think', is a non-factive verb. In non-factive verbs the truth value of the complement clause is not presupposed by the speaker. That's why 'it is raining' is not presupposed by the speaker and the statement

'I thought it was raining, but it was not.' is grammatical. Factive verbs such as know presuppose the truth value of the complement. 'I know it is raining but it is not' is ungrammatical. The factive verb doesn't allow negative raising. Therefore they are not ambiguous.

The occurrence of the verbal negative polarity expressions is significant from a typological perspective too. To the best of our knowledge neither Indo-Aryan languages nor Dravidian languages have such expression. Tibeto-Burman languages such as Mizo, Hmar, Angami, Manipuri too do not seem to have such expressions. Moreover, Ho, Santali, Mundari also do not seem to have it However, the occurrence of verbal negative polarity tense markers in addition to adverbial negative polarity items occurring together seems to be a very special feature of Rabha (Subbarao, 2002).

In Santali, negation is expressed by three particles (Neukom 1998)

a) ba, baa : negation of declarative and interrogative sentence

b) øhø : emphatice negation

c) alo : negated imperative

(82) ba-ko badae -a

neg-3pl know -IND

'They do not know.'

In Santali, the subject agreement marker is attached to the negative marker, which in turn immediately precedes the verb as like Ho. And in So:ra:, negation is indicated by the omission of tense marker *–l-* and *–t-*, and the addition of the prefix *ad-* or *er-*. But negation in the past tense is sometimes indicated merely by the prefix *ad-*: the tense marker *–l-* is not dropped.

In Mundari, *ka-* is general term for negative and is used both morphologically and syntactically. Thus, an affirmative indicative sentence may be changed to negative one by placing *ka-* immediately before the verb for the purpose of negating the action. And the subject agreement marker is added to this particle as like Ho. Interestingly, the negation marker *ka-* itself may be used as a verb in full personal construction in all tenses and moods, both transitively and intransitively as the followings:

(83) ka –iñ -keD -a -e
neg-1sg –pst –dec –3sg
'He said 'no' to me.'

Prohibitions are expressed by the use of a special particle *alo*, which is equivalent to 'do not' and is followed by the indicative future in Ho.

(84) alo-m giti-a
do not –2sg sleep-dec
'Do not sleep.'

15. Interrogatives

According to Greenberg (1966) universal 12, it is argued that ' If a language has dominant order VSO ...... interrogative words or phrases first in interrogative word questions; if it has dominant order SOV in declarative sentences, there is never such an invariant rule.' Thus question word remains in-situ in Ho.

(1)	(aben)$_i$	okona	-ben $_i$	seno	-tan	-a	?
	you.pol	*where*	*2dual*	*go*	*prog*	*dec*	

'Where are you going ?

(2)	en	-kui hon	-ko $_i$	okon /	okoe /	* okna	-ko $_i$?
	that	*Girl*	*pl*		*who*		*Ⅲpl*

'Who are those girls ?

(3)	pro $_i$	hola	ciken	-re-	-^{y}a	ka	-m $_i$	huju	-^{y}an	-a	?
	you	*yesterday*	*why*	*emph*	*emph*	*not*	*Ⅱsg*	*come*	*pst*	*dec*	

'Why didn't you come yesterday '

(4)	pro$_i$	okona /	*okon /	*okoe	dureŋ	-em $_i$	sanaŋ	-tan	-a	?
	you		*which*		*song*	*Ⅱsg*	*like*	*pres*	*dec*	*?*

'Which song do you like?'

As we can see from the examples above there is a distinction between animate *okon* or *okoe* and non-animate *okona* in (1) and (4). The distinction between the [±animate] in the interrogative construction is also respectable in Ho. But there seems to be no real distinction in conversation.

16. Position of yes/no and tag question markers

In Ho there is also yes/no question marker *cikana / cina* and they come to the beginning of the sentence as in *kya* does so in Hindi.

(5)	ciken-riya / cina	pro$_i$	pid	-re	-ben $_i$	seno	-tan	-a	?
	yes/no ques mkr		*market*	*in*	*Ⅱdual*	*go*	*prog*	*dec*	*?*

'Are you going to the market ?

(6)	pro$_i$	pid	-re	-ben $_i$	seno	-tan	-a	ci	?
	you	*market*	*in*	*Ⅱdual*	*go*	*prog*	*dec*	*tag*	*?*

'You are going to the market, aren't you ? '

In (6), *ci* functions as like a tag question marker. Thus it is not a yes/no question marker. Because sentences (5) and (6) are not same. And *ci* is also used for 'or' as well as complementizer 'that 'as followed in:

(7)	nen	topi	ci	en	topi	?
	this	*cap*	*or*	*that*	*cap*	*?*

'This cap or that cap ? '

(8)	añ	kaji – keD – a	ci	am $_i$	puti – ko – m $_i$	kiriŋ - keD –a
	I	*say pst dec*	*comp*	*you*	*book pl Ⅱsg*	*buy pst dec*

'I told that you bought books. '

As indicated earlier, questions in Ho are asked by adding *ci* to the end of a sentence although it functions as like a tag question. However sometimes merely the inflection of the voice indicates the question and no *ci* is put as the following:

(9)	pro$_i$	pid	-re	-ben $_i$	seno	-tan	-a	?
	you	*market*	*in*	*Ⅱdual*	*go*	*prog*	*dec*	

'You are going to the market ? '

To make a negative interrogative we can put ci immediately after the negative marker:

(10) pro_i ka -ci $-m_i$ seno $-^{w}a$? / ka -m seno $-^{w}a$ ci ?
you not –quest -2ng go -dec not –2sg go -dec tag
'Aren't you going?'

We give here some of the more common interrogative pronouns and adjectives. For pronouns we also give the dual and plural forms.

okoe	'who – a person'	okoetikiŋ	'who–dual'
okoeteko	'who –plural'	okoni	'whichone–animate'
okona	'which thing-inanimate'	okon	'which –adjective'
okonre	'in or on where'	onte	'towhere'
okonete	'from where'	chuila	'when'
chimin	'how much'	chilika	'how'
chikani	'what-animate'	chikankiŋ	'what–dual'
chikanko	'what-plural'	chikana	'what-inanimate'
chikanakiŋ	'what-dual'	chikanako	'what-plural'

In So:ra: interrogation is also expressed by the employment of appropriate particles, namely *pa* or *poŋ* occurs to the end of a sentence. In Santali, yes/no questions are marked by stress on the last syllable of the verb (Ghosh, 1992 quoted from Neukom 1998:47).

17. Anaphors

Ho also does not have nominal reflexives. It has only verbal reflexive device as like in Mundari and Santali which belong to Munda family.

Let us consider the following examples:

(11) pro_i añ-te-ge -ñ $_i$ goe$^?$ -ke -n -a

I me Isg kill pst [-tr] dec

'I killed myself. '

(12) pro_i añ-te -ñ $_i$ goe$^?$ -ken -a

I me-by Isg kill pst+VR dec

'I killed myself. '

(13) añ añ -ge citti ool -keD -a

I me emph letter write pst dec

'I wrote a letter to myself. '

(14) pro añ-ta$^?$a-re ram-iñ kul -ki$^?$ –^{y}e

I me -to Ram-1sg send –pst-3sg-dec

'I sent Ram to myself.'

I, here, claim that *añ-te-ge* is not a nominal reflexive form. Because , as we can see in (11-14), *añ* 'me' – recall that in Ho there is no different form between subject and object, and there is no accusative marker – is only a reduplicate form for emphasis and *–te* 'with' as well as *–ge* 'emphatic clitics' are optional. Even though a nominal device is optional in most of Dravidian languages due to the existence of verbal reflexives, Ho is not in that case.

If so, now we need to analyze the form of verbal reflexive in Ho. Is there a specific verbal reflexive marker? As we can see there seems to be no distinctive form of the VR in Ho. Furthermore, if we know that an intransitive marker is *–n* , then we may find that *–n* can be a VR as well as an intransitive marker and a passive marker due to the function of a detransitivizer. And the sentence (14) indicates that the reflexive marker can not occur when subject and indirect object are co-indexed. Thus, the sentence is [+transitivity].

Let us consider the following examples:

(15) pro $_i$ ø aRsi -re -m $_i$ nel -ke -n -a
you mirror in IIsg see pst [-tr] dec
'You saw yourself in the mirror. '

(16) pro $_i$ ø aRsi -re -m $_i$ nel -e -n -tan -a
you mirror in IIsg see epen [-tr] pres dec
'You see yourself in the mirror. '

(17) pro $_i$ añ -te -ge –ñ $_i$ toke -kie -n -a
I me with emph I sg hit pst [-tr] dec
'I hit mysef. '

(18) pro $_i$ añ -te -ge –ñ $_i$ toke -ta -n -a
I me with emph I sg hit -pres [-tr] dec
'I hit mysef '

Sentences (15) to (18) which show the simple past and present tense we can find the verbal reflexive form *–n*. We might guess that it is *–en*. But as an evidence in support of *–n* ① in (11) *–e* is the epenthesis and ② there is no agreement marker due to the detransitivizing effect of *–n*.

And the reciprocal marker *–p-* is infixed into the verb after the first syllable, namely *V1 + p-Vowel + V2 + Aux*. /-pV-/, where V is the preceding vowel, as infix is inserted into transitive roots after vowel and then the same vowel is made to follow before taking other phonemes of the original form as the following examples:

(19) ale $_i$ ce –pe –reb -ke -n -a -le $_i$
we V1 VREC V2 pst [-tr] dec I dual
'We kissed each other. '

(20)	alaŋ	ne	-pe	-l	-tan	-a
	we	*V1*	*VREC*	*V2*	*prog*	*dec*

'We are seeing each other. '

[8](21)	hon-ko $_i$	-ko $_i$	gi	-pi	-l	-tan	-a
	children	*IIIpl*	*V1*	*VREC*	*V2*	*prog*	*dec*

'The children are fighting each other. '

Even though there is a verbal reciprocal form in Ho there is no possessive reciprocal form due to the absence of nominal reciprocals and nominal reflexives. Thus, a detransitivizer *–n* cannot occur in (22)

(22)

pro$_i$	am-a	kiteb	-eñ $_i$	paRaaw	-keD-a	ondo	pro$_j$	kiteb	-em $_j$	paRaaw	keD-a
I	*your*	*book*	*I sg*	*read*	*pst dec*	*and*	*you*	*book*	*IIsg*	*read*	*pst dec*

'We read each other's book. '

The lexical Gap (or Haplology[9]) is found in Ho as shown in the following examples:

(23) alaŋ $_i$	a	-pa	-suraai	–ka	-n	–a	-laŋ $_i$
we	*V1*	*VREC*	*V2*	*pst*	*[-tr]*	*dec*	*I dual*

'We, two loved each other. '

(24) alaŋ $_i$	pro $_j$	apasuraai / *asuraai	–am $_j$	tan	–a	-laŋ $_i$
we	*you*	*love*	*IIsg*	*pres*	*dec*	*I dual*

'We love you. '

And there is no long distance binding in Ho. Because verbal reflexive is subject-oriented. Thus we cannot find any long distance binding.

---

[8] Here the subject agreement marker occurs to the subject.

[9] If this case is a haplology, probably the sentence must be *'alaŋ a-pa-pasuraai –kan–a-laŋ* '. However, we cannot find that data as an evidence.

Let us now look at more examples:

(25) a. pro$_i$ giti -ka -n -a -ko$_i$.

they sleep-pst –[-TR]-dec –3pl

'They slept.'

(25)b. pro$_i$ pro$_j$ cereb –ke –D -mi$_j$ -^{y}a -ñ$_i$

I you kiss -pst-[+TR] –2sg-dec -1sg

'I kissed you.'

(25)c. pro$_i$ ø aRsi -re -m$_i$ nel -ke -n -a.

you mirror in - IIsg see -pst –[-TR/VRM] -dec

'You saw yourself in the mirror. '

The above examples show that pronominal subjects are dropped due to the occurrence of the subject agreement marker, and that the form of the marker of [+transitivity] and a [-transitivity] are *–D* and *–n,* respectively. Although the verb in the sentence (25c) is a transitive verb *–nel* 'see', the intransitive marker *–n* occurs since it is a reflexive sentence. As I already mentioned in section 1, the marker *–n* in Ho is the verbal reflexive as well as the intransitive and the passive marker[10]in the past tense. This phenomenon may be quite related to the function of the detransitivization. We can find detransitivizing in many languages as the function of reflexives.

(26) soma$_i$ uRuu-ke-D-a ci ram$_j$ ø$_{*i/j}$ suku-n -tan-a

Soma think-pst-TR-dec that Ram self like-VRM-pres-dec

'Soma$_i$ thought that Ram$_j$ likes himself$_{*i/j}$.'

(27) soma$_i$ uRuu-ke-D-a ci ram$_j$ (a^{y}e$_i$-e$_j$) suku-^{w}e-tan-a

Soma think-pst-TR-dec that Ram him-3sg like-3sg-pres-dec

'Soma$_i$ thought that Ram$_j$ likes him$_{i/k/*j}$'

[10] The marker *–n* is not a homonymity. This might have multiple interpretations in both the semantics and the syntax.

As Lidz (2001:124) points out, the division into reflexivizing and nonreflexivizing anaphors is intended to capture the apparent antilocality of the nonreflexivizing ones. In (26) the verbal reflexive marker *–n* can refer to the embedded clause subject, *Ram* since the property of the verbal reflexive is subject-oriented[11] and reflexive marked predicates, i.e., complex anaphors, verbal reflexives and inherent lexical verbs, which are SELF anaphors, do not allow the long distance binding. When there is no verbal reflexive marker so that the matrix subject can be coindexed with the embedded clause object, the direct object must occur to the verb as a suffix as shown in (27). And the transitive marker *–D* must occur to the verb since the subordinate direct object $d^{y}e$ 'him', which is pronominal here, is not identical with its subordinate subject *Ram*.

It is not necessarily that the reflexive which, has the properties given by Cole & Sung, must be LD reflexive. Anyway let us see the case of the verbal reflexive in Ho. It also has the following properties:

i) is monomorphemic: the marker is *–n*, no nominal reflexive marker other than the verbal reflexive,
ii) is subject-orientated: it is well known that verbal reflexive is subject-orientated as Subbarao (1997, 2001) points out,
iii) manifests the blocking effect as observed in (16), which is repeated here:

(28) a. soma$_i$ uRuu-ke-D-a ci añ$_j$ pro$_{*i/j}$ suku-n-tan-a
Soma think-pst-tr-dec that I self like-VRM-pres-dec
'Soma$_i$ thought that I$_j$ like myself$_{*i/j}$.'

(28)b. soma$_i$ uRuu-ke-D-a ci ram$_j$ pro$_{*i/j}$ suku-n-tan-a
Soma think-pst-tr-dec that Ram self like-VRM-pres-dec
'Soma$_i$ thought that Ram$_j$ likes himself$_{*i/j}$.'

When the subordinate subject has the same feature as like the matrix subject, it always blocks the coindexation as found in (28).

---

[11] Subbarao (1997, 2001) argues that a verbal reflexive has the property of subject-orientation.

Now, let us examine the following sentence (29). If we look at that carefully, then we find that the verb is [+transitivity] but the intransitive marker *–n* occurs although it is not reflexive context because the object and the subject are not identical.

(29) ram$_i$ soma-ta$^?$are laD -e$_i$ ema-ki-n-^{y}a. (Deeney)
Ram Soma-to bread-3sg give-pst-[INTR]-dec
'Ram GAVE HIS bread to Soma.'

Here, we see the interesting relationship between the verbal reflexive marker and the direct object, which is not identical with a subject. According to Deeney (1966), in Ho grammar by transitive we mean object stressing (the action referred especially to the object) and by intransitive we mean action stressing (with less emphasis on any object although at times on may be expressed) and the possessive relationship. The subject *Ram* and the direct object *laD* 'bread' are not identical in (29), although the verbal reflexive marker (the intransitive marker) *–n* occurs. However, the relationship between two NPs is possessive as indicated in (29). And the focus of the context is to emphasis on the action and the possessive relationship. Anyway, the example (29) does not have the interpretation of 'Ram gave Soma$_i$ bread for himself$_i$.'.

(30) ram *pro* giyu -n -tan -a.
Ram shame-VRM-pres-dec
'Ram shames himself.'

(31a). ram *pro* tam-ki-n-a.
Ram hit-pst-VRM-sec
'Ram hit himself.'

(30b) ram$_i$ añ$_j$-^{y}e$_i$ tam- ki-D-iñ$_j$-a.
Ram me-3sg hit-pst-TR-1sg-dec
'Ram hit me.'

Sentences (30) and (31a) exhibit the verbal reflexive but not nominal devices. When the verbal reflexive marker appears to the verb, only *pro* can occur instead of that the non-overt direct object occurs in Ho (in some cases, but, the direct object (Referential expression) occur).

This is because of the detransitiving effect by the verbal reflexive. While there is no direct object agreement marker inside the verb in (31a) since the verbal reflexive marker absorbs the one of its argument (internal argument), and there is the object agreement marker *–iñ* in (31b) since the subject and the object are not coindexed so that the transitive marker *–D* must occur. We also find this null object in the reciprocal construction in Ho. And the transitive marker *–D* cannot occur due to the detransitivizing effect by the intransitive marker *–n*, which is also a reflexive marker and the absence of direct object which is a reflexive.

(32a). pro_i am_j mandi-m_j jom ti^ya-$ñ_i$ sanaŋ-ke-D-a.
I you rice-2sg eat to -1sg like-pst-TR-dec
'I wanted you [PRO to eat rice]'
'I wanted you to eat rice.'

(32b) * ram [pro mandi jom ti^ya]-e sanaŋ-ke-n-a
Ram rice eat to -3sg like-pst-VRM-dec
'Ram wanted pro [PRO to eat rice]'
'Ram wanted himself to eat rice.'

The following sentence (33) where pronoun occurs, is the possible way to have to-infinitival ECM construction with respect to the reflexivity in Ho.

(33) ram_i [a^ye-te-$ge_{i/j}$ mandi-$^ye_{i/j}$ jom ti^ya]-^we_i sanaŋ-ke-D-a
Ram him-by-emph rice -3sg eat to -3sg like-pst-TR-dec
'Ram wanted himself/him to eat rice.'

The sentence (33) indicates that the emphatic pronoun, *a^ye-te-ge* occurs instead of null object in reflexive context. Hence, instead the verbal reflexive marker *–n*, occurs, the transitive marker, *–D* occurs since the sentence is the transitivity and both subject and object are not identical. The sentence (34) shows the possible way to read both sloppy and strict interpretation. The sentence (34) where the predicate is lexically reflexive-marked, shows that both readings are available either by a verbal reflexive morpheme alone or by a complex anaphor.

(34a). ram$_i$ Ø aRsi-re$^?$-e$_i$ nel –ke -n –a.

Ram self mirror-in-3sg see-pst-VRM-dec

'Ram saw himself in the mirror.'

'Ram saw his reflection in the mirror.'

(34b). tam-ke-n-a-ñ

hit-pst-VRM-dec-1sg

'I hit myself (myself or the statue)

And this phenomenon may be related with the passive voice in Ho. Before we go to the passive voice, consider the following sentence, which does not allow a strict reading but does only a sloppy reading.

(35) pro$_i$ añ$_i$ –te -ge -ñ$_i$ nel –ke -n-a

I me-by-emph-1sg see-pst-VRM-dec

'I saw myself (= I, *statue).'

The sentence (35)[12] has only a sloppy interpretation.

Let us look at the following sentences:

(36a). ram$_i$ kule-te-ge-e$_i$ goe$^?$-ke-n-a.

Ram tiger-by-emph-3sg kill-pst-INTR-dec

'? Ram KILLED HIS tiger.'

'Ram is killed by a tiger.'

(36b) (añ)$_i$ añ-te-ge-ñ$_i$ goe$^?$-ke-n-a.

I me-by-emph-1sg kill-pst-INTR-dec

'I killed myself. (myself but not statue).'

'I was killed by myself (=me but not statue).'

---

[12] It is crucial point that *añ-te-ge* in (35) is not an NP but a PP since the postpostion *–te* 'by' always follows in this context. Let us consider the following example:

(a) pro añ –ge -ñ nel –ke -n-a
I me-emph-1sg see-pst-VRM-dec
'? I saw myself (= I, *statue).'

In normal reflexive contexts in Ho, no direct objects occur except in some sentences as like (36). Thus, (36a) is i) to stress action as well as the possessive relationship (I claim that, in a sense, this is an indirect reflexivizing way of the subject's possession) since the intransitive marker (reflexive marker) is used, and the direct object occur as the PP, and ii) to show the passive since the intransitive marker (passive marker) and the PP occurs. Anyway, both sentences (36a) and (36b) are also the passive sentence besides that they have also different interpretation.

Let us examine the following sentences:

(37) pro$_i$ Ø goe$_?$-ke-n-a-ñ$_i$.
I *kill-pst-INTR-dec-1sg*
'I killed myself (= myself or statue).'
'I was killed.'

(38) pro$_i$ ema-aka-n-a-ñ$_i$. (Burrows 1980)
I *give-pres.perf-INTR-dec-1sg*
'I was given.'
'I have given myself.'

We may ask how the intransitive marker *-n* can be used as the passive and the reflexive in Ho. If they are not homonymous, then how the sentence (38) can be interpreted as both the passive and the reflexive? Is it enough to answer that both are simply detransitivized. Let us look at the following sentence, which contains the indirect object:

(39) pro$_i$ Ø siŋboŋga-ta?a-re-m$_i$ ema-ke-n-a.
you *God -to-in-2sg* *give-pst-INTR-dec*
'You gave yourself to the God.'
'You were given to the God.'

In a sense, semantically, the meaning of the passive is very similar with the meaning of the reflexive as shown in (39). Who was dedicated to the God? That is 'you' in both contexts.

And the direct object agreement marker never occurs in both sentences due to the deransitivizing effect. This detransitivizing effect is also found in the causative constructions when the direct object and the subject are identical. Let us look at the causative construction in Ho as follows:

(40a) pro$_i$ kubiraj- ta?a-re-ñ$_i$ Ø nel –ici -ke -n-a.
I doctor -to-in-1sg see –causative-pst-VRM-dec
'I showed myself to a doctor.'

(41b) ram$_i$ añ- ta?a-ete-e$_i$ Ø giti-ici-ke-n-a
Ram me-to-by-3sg sleep-causative-pst-VRM-dec
'Ram made me put himself to sleep.'

In Ho, there is no correspondent word for 'show'. So, they use the causative construction as seen in (40a). In (40), anyway, no direct object can occur since both sentences are detransitivized by the verbal reflexive marker. Instead, only NPs which are headed by the postposition can occur, but these PP are not identical with the subject.

However the verbal reflexive cannot refer to the indirect object as exampled in (41) and (42). This implies the property of the subject-orientation.

(41a) goe$^?$ –n –me. (Deeney1966)
kill –VRM-imperative
'Kill yourself.'

(41b) puti$_i$ ema-e$_i$-me.
book give –3sg-imperative
'Give a book.'

(41c) *puti$_i$ ema-e$_i$-n-me.
book give-3sg-VRM-imperative
'Give a book to yourself.'

(42) puti ema-ko-me.

book give-3pl-imperative

'Give a book to them.'

In imperative constructions, the subject is always the second person. The suffix –me is the agreement marker of 2nd singular. Thus, the direct object is only identified with the 2nd person in the imperative reflexive contexts. As illustrated in (41c), it cannot be identical with the indirect object. Because, as Subbarao (1997 and 2001) points out, the verbal reflexive has the property of subject orientation.

But, when there is an intervening NP, mostly an direct object in the reflexive context, the verbal reflexive cannot be identical with the subject and the passive interpretation is not available in Ho. Only possible interpretation is that is has the action stressing and possessive relationship as shown in (43a). Apart from the identity, the emphatic reflexive is used with the pronominal as illustrated in (43c). However, the verbal reflexive marker/the intransitive marker cannot occur in such contexts. Instead, the transitive marker –D occurs. So the direct object marker –iñ has to occur into the verb.

(43a) añ$_i$ ciTTi-ñ$_i$ ool-la-n-a.

I letter write-pst.perf-INTR-dec

'* I wrote a letter to myself.'

' I WROTE MY letter.'

'* I was written by a letter.'

(43b) añ$_i$ añ-ta$^?$a-re ciTTi-ñ$_i$ ool –la -D-a.

I me-to-in letter-1sg write-pst.perf-TR-dec

'I wrote a letter to myself.'

(43c) siŋboŋga$_i$ pro$_j$ a^{y}e-lageD-ge$^?$-e$_i$ bai-ke-D-iñ$_j$-ya.

God me him-for-emph-3sg creat-pst-TR-1sg-dec

'A god created me for him/himself.'

(44a) pro$_i$ Ø$_i$ nel-ke -n -a -ñ$_i$.

I see-pst-VRM-dec-1sg

'I saw myself (= I or statue).'

(44b) pro$_i$ añ$_i$ –te -ge -ñ$_i$ nel –ke -n-a

I me-by-emph-1sg see-pst-VRM-dec

'I saw myself (= I, *statue).'

It is also important to see that the verbal reflexive marking does not represent a deleted indirect object in Ho. As we have seen, an indirect object cannot be coreferent with the subject in verbal reflexive sentences. The occurrence of the indirect object, which is identical with the subject, does not allow the occurrence of the verbal reflexive marker in Ho. Instead, the transitive marker must occur. This is because that there is no nominal device in Ho. Instead, the use of the pronominal can substitute the nominal anaphor. Let us look at the following sentences:

(45a) añ$_i$ añ$_i$-ta$^?$a-re haku$_j$-ñ$_i$ ema-ke-D-e$_j$-^{w}a

I myself-to-in fish-1sg give-pst-TR-3sg-dec

'I gave a fish to myself.'

(45b) añ$_i$ Ø*$_i$ haku-ñ$_i$ ema-ke-n-^{w}a

I myself fish-1sg give-pst-VRM-dec

* ' I gave a fish to myself.'

'I GAVE MY fish (to someone).'

(45c) pro$_i$ abung-ke-n-a-ñ$_i$ (Deeney1966)

wash- past-INTR-dec-1sg

'I washed myself.'

'I washed MY feet and hands'

(45d) pro$_i$ rasa-n-tan-a-ñ$_i$.

enjoy-VRM-pres-dec-1sg

'I am enjoying myself'

The sentence in (45a) shows the possible way to have the indirect object which is identical with the subject since the pronominal for 'I' occurs. So, we also find the direct object agreement marker *–e* on the verb since the transitive marker *–D* requires the object agreement marker. However, the sentence (45b) does not have the interpretation of 'I gave a fish to myself' since it is impossible to coindex between the subject and the indirect object in the reflexive contexts.

We may think that the occurrence of the verbal reflexive marker indicates the coindexation between the subject and the indirect object if the direct object occurs. However, as we have observed earlier, it is not true that they are identical. Instead, it has the different interpretation 'I GAVE MY fish' as shown in (45b).

There are no reciprocal pronouns in So:ra:. The particle *al-* or *ar-* is prefixed to the verbal forms to express reciprocity.

(46) anin	-ji	al	-tid	-te	-ji
he	*-3pl*	*recipro*	*–beat*	*–pres*	*–3pl*

'They are beating each other.'

So:ra: has no word corresponding to self. There is no nominal anaphor. Instead, the emphatic and reflexive senses of this word are expressed. Namely, the particle *–na* expresses emphasis here and the particle *–dƏm* is used for the reflexivity as following:

(47a)	anin	–na	gij	-ete	-n
	he	*emph*	*see*	*–pst*	*-3sg*

'He saw himself.'

(47b)	anin	po:	-dƏm	-n	-ete	-n
	he	*stab*	*VRM*		*-pst*	*-3sg*

'He stabbed himself.'

Let us look at some examples from Santali.

(47c)	pro	dal	-a	-e
	he	*strike*	*IND*	*–3sg*

'He will strike.'

(47d) pro dal -og -ok -a -e

he strike redulication -VRM -IND -3sg

'He will strike himself.'

The sentence (47c) shows that there is a verbal reflexive marker *-ok* but it is reduplicated by *–og* in Santali. And the reciprocal stem is formed by infixing *–pV-* after the first vowel, *V* adopts the same vowel quality as the preceding vowel as exactly like as Ho. And Mundari has the verbal reflexive marker as like Ho.

Thus, in [-past] tense, the verbal reflexive marker *–n-* occurs to the verb as an infix and in [+past] tense, the intransitive marker which is a verbal reflexive marker *–n* occurs instead of occurring of *D* 'transitive marker'. Moreoever, the reciprocal forms are used as like Ho and Santali.

18. Cleft

Clefts are not permitted in Ho. As mentioned earlier there is no corresponding form for 'it' in Ho. The example below shows a relative clause.

(48)

ini$^{?}{}_{i}$	ashi	-ge	min	-a	-^{y}e $_{i}$	okoi	jom	-keD	-a	(-i)$_{i}$
he	*Ashi*	*emph*	*is*	*dec*	*IIIsg*	*who*	*eat*	*pst*	*dec*	*IIIsg*

'He is a Ashi who ate.'

19. Ergativity

Ho language does not exhibit any ergativity at all. It is a Nom–Acc language.

(49)	(añ)$_{i}$	kui-hon	-ko $_{j}$	–ñ $_{i}$	nel	–aD	-ko $_{j}$	–a	-ø $_{i}$
	I	*girl*	*pl*	*Isg*	*see*	*pst.pef*	*IIIpl*	*dec*	*Isg*

'I had seen girls.'

(50)	(añ)$_{i}$	kui-hon	-ko $_{j}$	-ø	nel	-aD	-ko $_{j}$	-a	-ñ $_{i}$
	I	*girl*	*pl*		*see*	*pst.pef*	*IIIpl*	*dec*	*Isg*

'I had seen girls.'

In (49) it seems that the ergative case marker is ø because there is only direct object agreement (DO Agr) inside verb. But in Ho subject agreement (Sub Agr) prefers to occur to the preverbal position rather than to the end of verb. So in (50) we can see both Sub Agr and DO Agr inside the verb.

20. Agreement

Ho language is very rich in agreement. And we can see agreement in terms of [±animate] and the thematic hierarchy. And Ho language also shows that lexical case marking blocks the agreement. However, according to Subbarao, a noun phrase whether lexically case marked or not agrees with the verb if the functional head agreement is "active". Agreement is not morphologically manifested and is "covert" if the functional head agreement is "weak".

For the sake of clarity this part has been divided into many sections. And most of agreements in this topic is related to the pro-drop phenomenon. This heavy pro-drop language is due to the rich agreement. There is an attempt to show how subject agreement marker can be suffixed to preverbal constituent according to the concept of merge under minimalist program, and anti-symmetry. And there are some studies of the agreement patterns in many situations in Ho. And we will discuss that agreement marker also has extra functions. Moreover we will also discuss the relation between the occurrence of the agreement and thematic role in Ho.

Agreement in [-transitive] verbs

It has been established so far that a subject of a [-transitive] verb is either unmarked when agreement marker occurs into the verb or marked when there is no subject agreement marker in the verb. That is to say, if there is no constituent other than a subject and a verb[13], the pronominal subject is optional in accordance with the occurrence of subject agreement marker. And subject agreement marker can occur even though a subject is not dropped.

(51) abu $_i$	seno	-ø	-a	(-bu)$_i$	=	pro $_i$	seno	-a	-bu $_i$
we	*go*	*fut*	*dec*	*1pl*		*we*	*go*	*dec*	*1pl*

'We will go. '

[13] The preferable position of the occurrence of subject agreement marker is the preverbal constituent position in Ho. We will discuss this point in detail later.

(52) ako $_i$ giti -ka -n -a (-ko)$_i$ = pro $_i$ giti -kan -a -ko $_i$

they sleep pst [-tr] dec Ⅲpl

'They have slept '

(53) duwer $_i$ handed -^{y}e -n -a (*i / *e) $_{*i}$

door close pst [-tr] dec Ⅲsg

'The door closed '

[14](54) kuihon –ko $_i$ giti -tan -a -ko $_i$

girl pl sleep prog dec Ⅲpl

'The girls are sleeping '

In (53) there is no subject agreement marker because of the [-animate] subject while in (54) the subject agreement marker occurs because of the [+animate] subject.

Agreement in [+transitive] verbs

Ho is a Nom-Acc type language. The pronominal subject and object of a [+transitive] verb are heavily dropped due to the presence of subject and object agreement markers.

And direct object agreement marker also occurs in accordance with the [±animate] and [±past] tense. We will discuss this point later later.

(55) pro $_i$ laD $_j$ -iñ $_i$ jom -e $_j$ -ø -^{y}a

I bread I sg eat Ⅲsg fut dec

'I will eat bread. '

(56) pro $_i$ ladD $_j$ -iñ $_i$ jom -ke -D -ø $_j$ -a

I bread I sg eat pst [+tr] Ⅲsg dec

'I ate bread. '

[14] The plural maker and 3 rd person plural pronominal agreement markers are same in Ho.

(57)	pro $_i$	laD $_j$	-iñ $_i$	jom	-e $_j$	-tan	-a
	I	*bread*	*I sg*	*eat*	*IIIsg*	*pres/prog*	*dec*

'I am eating bread / I eat bread. '

(58)	pro $_i$	laD $_j$	-iñ $_i$	jom	-ø $_{*j}$	-dai	-ø $_{*j}$	-^{y}a
	I	*bread*	*I sg*	*eat*	*IIIsg*	*can*	*IIIsg*	*dec*

'I can eat bread. '

(59)	siima $_i$	a^{y}e	-$^?$a	manDi	-i $_i$	jom	-ke	-D	-a
	Sema	*she*	*gen*	*meal*	*IIIsg*	*eat*	*pst*	*[+tr]*	*dec*

'Sema had her meal. '

From (55) to (58) we can understand that pronominal subjects are dropped due to the occurrence of the agreement marker to the second constituent, namely the preverbal position. And also direct object agreement occurs to the verb as a suffix in [-past] tense since the direct object is [-animate]. However the following examples show the occurrence of direct object agreement in the verb as well as the occurrence of subject agreement in the direct object when DO is not dropped, and in the verb when DO is dropped, respectively.

(60)	pro $_i$	am $_j$	-eñ $_i$	cereb	-ke	-D	-mi $_j$	-^{y}a	-ø
	I	*you*	*I sg*	*kiss*	*pst*	*[+tr]*	*IIsg*	*dec*	

'I kissed you. '

(61)	pro $_i$	pro $_j$	cereb	-ke	-D	-mi $_j$	-^{y}a	-ñ $_i$
	I	*you*	*kiss*	*pst*	*[+tr]*	*IIsg*	*dec*	*I sg*

'I kissed you. '

In (60) the subject agreement occurs to the right of the direct object which occupies the preverbal position. And in (61) where the subject and object both are dropped, the subject agreement comes to the end of the sentence as like in [-transitive] cases, and the object agreement occurs to the right of the transitive marker. But the latter sentence (61) is the unmarked sentence when subject and object are pronouns in Ho. That means that this language is a heavy pro-drop language.

Agreement in ditransitive verbs

As we have seen the order of DO and IO in the part 2, the unmarked sentence in Ho is Sub + IO + DO + V + Aux. The subject agreement is, of course, suffixed to preverbal word. The direct object agreement marker cannot occur in the verb if the indirect object is not lexically case marked[15] but occurs in the verb if the indirect object is lexically case marked. However an indirect object pronoun is also heavily dropped if it is not lexically case marked as in the following examples:

(62a) pro$_i$ pro$_j$ mi^{y}ed' uli$_x$ –ñ$_i$ em– a– m$_j$ –tan –a
I you one mango Isg give epen IIsg prog dec
'I am giving you one mango. '

(62b) pro$_i$ pro$_j$ mi^{y}ed' uli$_x$ –ñ$_i$ em– aD- mi$_j$ -^{y}a
I you one mango Isg give pst.pef IIsg dec
'I had given you a mango. '

In the above sentences indirect objects are not lexically case marked. So the agreement marker must occur in the verb. Instead, the direct object agreement marker cannot come to the verb.

(62c) pro$_i$ añ$_x$–ta$^?$a kui-hon- ko$_j$ kul– keD– ko$_j$ -^{w}a– ben$_i$
you.polite me near girl pl send pst IIIpl dec IIdual
'You sent girls to me. '

(63) pro$_i$ gel kui-hon -ko$_j$ gara$_x$–re -ñ$_i$ em –ko$_j$ -tan -a
I ten girl pl river to Isg give IIIpl prog dec
'I am giving ten girls to the river. '

(64) pro$_i$ gel kui-hon -ko$_j$ gara$_x$ -re -ñ$_i$ em -akaD –ko$_j$ -a
I ten girl pl river to Isg give pres pef IIIpl dec
'I have given ten girls to the river. '

---

15 In Ho there is neither accusative nor dative marker as we have seen eariler.

As I already mentioned if an indirect object is not lexically case marked, a direct object agreement marker must occur in the verb. The indirect object is lexically cased marked by the postposition *–ta$^{?}$a* 'near'. Thus instead of the occurrence of the IO Agr marker in the verb, the 3rd plural direct object agreement marker *–ko* comes to the verb. The sentence (63) and (64) also show the same pattern.

The above sentences just show in the case where the direct object is not a pronoun. Because a direct object is weak in case of [-animate]. So we may wonder about the case that a subject, a direct object and an indirect object are all pronouns. Let us consider the following examples:

(65) pro $_i$ pro $_j$ a^{y}e -ñ $_i$ em -aD -mi $_j$ -^{y}a

I you he I sg give pst.pef IIsg dec

'I had given him to you. '

(66) pro $_i$ pro $_j$ ako -m $_i$ em -aD -iñ $_j$ -^{y}a

you me them IIsg give pst.pef I sg dec

'You had given them to me. '

Even though a direct object is a pronoun, the DO agreement does not occur in the verb in (65) and (66). We will see the reason and the hierarchy of agreement in the following section.

Agreement and adverb

Adverbs occur to the right of the subject in unmarked sentence. And subject agreement marker can occur to the right of adverb as a suffix as in (67).

(67) pro $_i$ mundo –ete -ñ$_i$ huju -tan -a

I school from I sg come prog dec

'I am coming from the school. '

(68a) pro $_i$ baamai –ete –ñ $_i$ jiliŋ –a

I Bamai than I sg tall dec

'I am taller than Bamai. '

(68b) sita $_i$ somi -ete –i $_i$ ceehra – ge –^{y}a

Sita Somi than IIIsg beautiful emph dec

'Sita is more beautiful than Somi. '

(68c) pro $_i$ jono -te seta $_j$ -ko $_i$ tam -ki$^{?}$ –i $_j$ - -^{y}e

they broom with dog IIIpl hit pst IIIsg dec

'They hit the dogs with the broom. '

The normal constituent order of VP of Ho is ADJUNCT – IO – DO – V. Hence the position in which any constituent occurs to the left of a verb is the first appropriate position for subject agreement marker.

Agreement markers and pro-drop

Ho is a very heavy pro-drop language. This, of course, is related to agreement. But there is a restriction of pro-drop that if subject, direct object and indirect object are all pronoun we cannot drop direct object pronoun. It is due to this reason that there is a thematic agreement hierarchy inside verb and subject agreement occurs to the right of preverbal position where direct object normally occurs in Ho.

These are subject agreement markers as well as direct object and indirect object agreement markers as being shown in below table. But there is no distinction between subject AGR and IO, DO AGR in Ho[16]. And 3rd person pronominal agreement marker are also used for [-human] nouns. Here these agreement markers might be formed from the copy of each pronoun after dropping *a-*.

<table>
<tr><th>AGR</th><th>Singular</th><th colspan="2">Dual</th><th colspan="2">Plural</th></tr>
<tr><td rowspan="2">1 st</td><td rowspan="2">-ñ/-iñ /-eñ</td><td>Incl [+you]</td><td>-laŋ</td><td>Incl [+you]</td><td>-bu</td></tr>
<tr><td>Excl [-you]</td><td>-liŋ</td><td>Excl [-you]</td><td>-le</td></tr>
<tr><td>2 nd</td><td>-m /-mi /-em</td><td colspan="2">-ben</td><td colspan="2">-pe</td></tr>
<tr><td>3 rd</td><td>-i /-e</td><td colspan="2">-kin</td><td colspan="2">-ko</td></tr>
</table>

16 We may ask why there are several forms of 1st, 2nd and 3rd singular in Ho. It seems that 1st and 2nd Agr are due to the vowel harmony or epenthesis and 3rd AGR is due to two types of pronouns, namely *ini* and ***a^{y}e***. So the end of each pronoun can be formed for AGR as like the pattern of the dual and plural pronouns.

(69) raam$_{i}$ siita$_{j}$ -lo$^{?}$o kiteb paRaaw -keD -a -kin$_{i+j}$

Ram Sita with book read pst dec Ⅲpl

'Ram read the book with Sita.'

(70) pro$_{i}$ am$_{j}$ -lo$^{?}$o kiteb paRaaw -keD -a -laŋ$_{i+j}$

I you with book read pst dec I dual[+you]

'I read the book with you.'

(71) pro$_{i}$ am$_{j}$ -lo$^{?}$o seno -ø -a -laŋ$_{i+j}$

I you with go fut dec I dual

'I will go with you.'

The above examples show that even though subject is a singular its agreement marker appears as a dual form when subject is presented with oblique object. Thus we could understand pro-drop subject with the help of existence of agreement markers though its agreement marker is presented as an incorporated form.

Subject Agreement in the preverbal position.

In Ho when there is any word other than verb and subject in a sentence, that is to say, if there is any constituent between verb and subject, agreement marker must move to the end of the that constituent. In other word when any word precedes the verb, subject agreement markers are suffixed to that word. In case of no word preceding, they are added to the declarative marker as a suffix.

(72) pro$_{i}$ cikan –a -m$_{i}$ jom -keD -a ?

you what epen Ⅱsg eat pst dec

'What did you eat ?'

(73) pro$_{i}$ uli ka -ñ$_{i}$ jom -keD -a

I mango not I sg eat pst dec

'I did not eat a mango.'

Sentences (72) and (73) show that subject agreement markers must be suffixed to the preverbal constituents.

Here we need to consider Kayne's Antisymmetry to get a correct constituent order. Because the normal constituent order within the VP of an SOV language is 'Adjunct-IO-DO-V' in Ho. According to Jayaseelan the Larson's proposal about VP is really consistent only with Kayne's claim that SPEC-HEAD-COMPLEMENT order is the structure of maximal phrases universally.

If we hold on to the SPEC-COMP-HEAD order for Ho language[17] which is a SOV language, we cannot generate the normal constituent order of Ho. Moreover this adoption is very useful to explain the phenomenon of agreement in preverbal position in Ho.

(74) siita $_i$	hola	raam $_j$	mi^{y}ed'	puti	–e $_i$	em-	aD-	i $_j$	-^{y}a
Sita	*yesterday*	*Ram*	*one*	*book*	*IIIsg*	*give*	*pst.pef*	*IIIsg*	*dec*

'Sita had given Ram a book yesterday. '

In Ho there are two positions where subject agreement can occur. One is inside verb when there is no other constituent other than subject and verb, and the other is preverbal position. It is kind of difficult to explain how subject agreement can occur in preverbal position.

However here I will try to explain that phenomenon in two different ways. One way will be explained by the concept of merge under minimalist program. And second one will be done by movement under anti-symmetry. Moreover I do not take the level of D-Structure. Because D-structure notion has a problem with thematic roles.

First of all, let us make a numeration set for sentence (74) as shown in below:

N = { sitta , hola, raam , mi^{y}ed' puti, em-aD-i-^{y}a , [+Sub Agr], [+tense], [+IO Agr] etc }

The above model shows that we, first, select *mi ^{y}ed' puti* 'one book' and *em-aD-i -^{y}a* 'gave'.Of course the verb is already fully-inflected in the lexicon, so it contains [+Sub Agr]feature, [+tense]feature, [+IO Agr]feature etc except morphological

17 Actually there is a claim that Munda language family is Sepe-Head-Complement . Moreover there is a sort of evidence for this claim. In some genitive structure head noun is governed from right to left in Ho.

elements for agreement markers and tense marker such as *-aD*, *-i* and *-ʸa* in (24). Thus before the verb *em* 'give' is merged with direct object it must be merged with each morphological elements. And we merge *mi'ʸed' puti* and *em-aD-i-ʸa* as like 1st step. Then this 1st step is also merged with *raam* 'Ram'.

These 1st ,2nd, 3rd and 4th merges can check each thematic role, feature and Case e.g. at 2st merge step, *raam* 'Ram' can get thematic role as a Recipient, and [+IO Agr] feature as well as [+dative Case]feature are deleted or checked off. But we should work another merge at the same time for multiple spell-out. The subject agreement marker must be merged with preverbal constituent.

Let us now turn to the movement case under anti-symmetry. The reason why we adopt anti-symmetry is that the rightward movement has some problems under the Spec-Complement-Head configuration when the agreement marker moves to the SPEC position, whereas the leftward movement does not so undr the Spec-Head-Comp configuration.

It illustrates that only the subject agreement marker *–e* raised to Spec of $Agr_{DO}P$ which it is preverbal position. But the subject agreement marker must be copied before moving to Spec position since verb should move up to the head of TP for checking or deleting all features and Case by Spec-Head relation.

However we may raise the question about how Head of VP3 has subject agreement element. To support this argument we need to assume that every V inside VP-shell can have visible morphological agreement markers as well as features.

As we can see from the tree diagram above each Spec-Head relation can give or inherently has agreement and feature though it is under VP-Shell. That is to say, the relation between Spec of VP1 and V bears [+DO] feature and agreement, another relation between Spec of VP2 and V also gives [+IO] feature and agreement, last relation between Spec and VP1 gives [+Sub] feature and agreement. Thus whenever V moves to another V position it can accumulate other features and agreements.

Then before V moves to the Head of $Agr_{DO}P$ subject agreement must be copied and then move to the Spec of $Agr_{DO}P$ as illustrated in below diagram. The reason for copying subject agreement marker is that V continuously raises to T position.

Thus Case and Feature and Agreement features can be checked off and deleted by every movement to each Head position. But there is still problem that how V of VP1 has Tense feature and how subject agreement marker can adjunct to the right of the Agr_{DO} instead of the left of the Agr_{DO}.

Though I discussed two different ways to explain the phenomenon of the occurrence of subject agreement marker to the preverbal position, they cannot be proper approaches. I admit that it still remains several problems.

However the other evidence for Sub agreement in preverbal position is that subject with emphatic clitics clearly carry subject agreement marker. Apart from the fact that [+human] subject can carry Sub agreement immediately after subject, emphatic clitics occurred after subject is also regarded as a preverbal word in an intransitive verb as the following examples:

$añ_i$ -^{y}o -$ñ_i$ jom -dai -a
I *emph* *I sg* *eat* *can* *dec*
' I also can eat '

$añ_i$ -^{y}o -ge -$ñ_i$ jom -dai -a
I *emph* *emph* *I sg* *eat* *can* *dec*
' I also can eat, too '

Tense and Agreement

In occurring and forming the object agreement markers we must first see whether the object is animate or inanimate, as well as whether [18]tense is [-past] or [+past].

---

[18] The [-past] tense contains future, present and present continuous while the [+past] tense does simple past, present perfect and past perfect.

Tense markers

Here we see briefly each [19]tense marker for the position of object agreement. As we already observed earlier, there is a transitive marker and intransitive marker, and those are *–D* and *–n* respectively.

Tense \ Verb	Transitive Verb	Intransitive Verb
Future	*ø*	*Ø*
Present	*-tan*	*-tan*
Present Continuous	*-tan*	*-tan*
Past Continuous	*-tan tai ken*	*-tan tai ken*
Simple Past	*-keD*	*-ken* / ^{y}*en*
Present Perfect	*-akaD*	*-akan*
Past Perfect	*-leD* / *-laD*	*-len*

Position of Object Agreement in relation with Tense

In unmarked sentence the normal order is that subject agreement marker always occurs to the right of the preverbal word and object agreement marker occurs to the either left of the tense marker or right of that marker in different cases due to the [±past] tense and the [±animate] object.

Tense	Preverbal word	Occurrence of DO Agr marker	When object is
[- past]	+ Sub Agr	V + DO Agr + tense mrk + *a*	[±animate]
[+past]		V + tense mrk + DO Agr + *a*	[+animate]
		V + tense mrk + ø + *a*	[-animate]

[19] In fact the distinction between tense and aspect is not clear in Ho.

(75) pro $_i$ ladD $_j$ -iñ $_i$ jom -ke -D -ø $_{*j}$ -a

I bread I sg eat pst [+tr] Ⅲsg dec

'I ate bread. '

(76) pro $_i$ laD $_j$ -iñ $_i$ jom -e $_j$ -tan -a

I bread I sg eat Ⅲsg pres/prog dec

'I am eating bread / I eat bread. '

(77) pro $_i$ laD $_j$ -iñ $_i$ jom -ø $_{*j}$ -dai -ø $_{*j}$ -^{y}a

I bread I sg eat Ⅲsg can Ⅲsg dec

'I can eat bread. '

In (76) direct object agreement marker occurs to the left of the tense marker while in (75) where tense is [+past] it did not occur. And DO agreement also does not seem to occur in (77) where auxiliary verb comes with the verb.

(78) pro $_i$ am $_j$ -eñ $_i$ cereb -ke -D -mi $_j$ -^{y}a -ø

I you I sg kiss pst [+ tr] Ⅱsg dec I sg

'I kissed you. '

(79) pro $_i$ pro $_j$ cereb -ke -D -mi $_j$ -^{y}a -ñ $_i$

I you kiss pst [+tr] Ⅱsg dec I sg

'I kissed you. '

(80) pro $_i$ pro $_j$ cereb -me $_j$ -tan -a -ñ $_i$

I you kiss Ⅱsg pres dec I sg

'I kiss you.'

Unlike the case in which Object is [-animate], DO agreement must occur when DO is [+animate] in Ho. And when tense is [+past] DO agreement occurs to the right of the verb while it occurs to the left of the verb in [-past] tense sentence.

(81) pro $_i$ añ $_j$ –em $_i$ cereb -ke -D -iñ $_j$ -^{y}a -ø

you me Ⅱsg kiss pst [+tr] I sg dec

'You kissed me. '

(82) pro $_i$ pro $_j$ cereb -ke -D -iñ $_j$ -^{y}a -m $_i$

you me kiss pst [+tr] I sg dec IIsg

'You kissed me. '

When both a direct object and an indirect object are pronouns an indirect object is usually appeared with postposition *–ta$^?$a* 'near' ,or a direct object is not dropped. And DO agreement and IO agreement cannot occur together. Here the occurrence of either DO agreement or IO agreement is also observed with relevance to the [±animate] object in [+past] tense.

Tense	Preverbal word	Occurrence of DO or IO Agr	Lexical case marking
[-past]	+ Sub Agr	V + IO Agr + tense mrk+ *a*	IO is not lexically case marked
		V + DO Agr + tense mrk + *a*	IO is lexically case marked (for-dative[20])
[+past]	+ Sub Agr	V + tense mrk + IO Agr + *a*	IO is not lexically case marked
		V + tense mrk + DO Agr + *a*	IO is lexically case marked (for-dative)

(83) pro $_i$ pro $_j$ gel kui-hon –ko $_x$ –ñ $_i$ em– a– m $_j$ -tan –a

I you ten girl pl I sg give epen IIsg prog dec

'I am giving you ten girls. '

(84) pro $_i$ pro $_j$ gel kui-hon –ko $_x$ –ñ $_i$ em– aD mi $_j$ –^{y}a

I you ten girl pl I sg give pst.pef IIsg dec

'I had given ten girls to you. '

Th sentences (83) and (84) illustrate the occurrence of indirect object agreement marker to the left of the verb and to the right of the verb respectively. However if indirect object is lexically case marked, direct object agreement occurs as the following examples:

[20] Though there is no dative case marker (to-dative) we can find for-dative indirect object in Ho.

(85a) pro$_{i}$ añ$_{x}$ –ta$^{?}$a kui-hon- ko$_{j}$ kul– keD– ko$_{j}$ -^{w}a– ben$_{i}$

you.polite me near girl pl send pst Ⅲpl dec Ⅱdual

'You sent girls to me.'

(85b) pro$_{i}$ pro$_{j}$ ako -m$_{i}$ em -aD -iñ$_{j}$ -^{y}a

you me them Ⅱsg give pst.pef Ⅰsg dec

'You had given them to me.'

The Role of [±animate] and [±human]

As I already mentioned that Ho is not concerned with gender, there is no any agreement with gender. But Ho is very much concerned with the [±animate][21].

The inanimate has only one marker *–e* / *-i* for the object in [-past] tense. There is only singular form for the inanimate standing for 'it'. However 3rd plural marker *–ko* can be used as an agreement marker for inanimate nouns.

(86) pro$_{i}$ uri$_{j}$ -iñ$_{i}$ kumbu -i$_{j}$ -tan -a

I cow Ⅰsg steal Ⅲsg pres dec

'I steal the cow.'

(87) pro$_{i}$ uri$_{j}$ -iñ$_{i}$ kumbu -ki -$^{?}$$_{j}$ -^{y}a

I cow Ⅰsg steal pst+Ⅲsg dec

'I stole the cow.'

When tense is [-past] [+animate] direct object agreement marker occurs to the left of the tense marker as in (86). And in (87) where tense is [+past] DO agreement is not clearly appeared. So we may find the distinction [±human]. Actually the occurrence of subject agreement marker to the right of the subject depends on [±human]. However in DO agreement cases there is no distinction between the two as shown in (88).

---

[21] According to An Introduction to the Ho language, the distinction between [±animate] is as followed that: [+animate] god, spirits, people, animals, the sun, moon and stars. [-animate] all other things including plants and trees. But I cannot find such kind of distinction from field work.

(88) a^{y}e$^{?}$$_{i}$ am -a seta –ko$_{j}$ -i$_{i}$ tam -ki$^{?}$ -ko$_{j}$ -^{y}e

he you gen dog pl IIIsg hit pst IIIpl dec

'He hit your dog.'

(89) am$_{i}$ kaji -keD -a ci pro$_{i}$ añ$_{j}$ -em$_{i}$ nel -aD -iñ$_{j}$ -a

you say pst dec comp you me IIsg see pst,pef I sg dec

'You said that you had seen me.'

However the examples below clearly indicate that [-animate] DO agreement cannot occur in the [+past] tense whereas it occurs to the left of the tense marker in the [-past] tense.

(90) pro$_{i}$ poesa$_{j}$ -ñ$_{i}$ kumbu -i$_{j}$ -tan -a

I money I sg steal IIIsg pres dec

'I steal the money.'

(91) pro$_{i}$ poesa$_{j}$ -ñ$_{i}$ kumbu -ki -ø -a

I money I sg steal pst dec

'I stole the money.'

(92) am$_{i}$ kaji -keD -a ci pro$_{i}$ puti –ko$_{j}$ -m$_{i}$ kiriŋ -keD -ø -a

you say pst dec comp you book pl IIsg buy pst dec

'You said that you bought books.'

The sentences (93) and (94) clearly show the occurrence of DO agreement between [±animate] objects.

(93) sema$_{i}$ upniye dasi -ko$_{j}$ kiriŋ -keD -ko$_{j}$ -^{w}a

Sema four servant pl buy pst IIIpl dec$_{i}$

'Sema bought four servants.'

(94) sema$_{i}$ upniye puti -ko$_{j}$–e kiriŋ -keD (-*ko$_{j}$) -^{w}a

Sema four book pl 3sg buy pst IIIpl dec

'Sema bought four books.'

Now let us have a look at the role of [±human]. In this case only subject agreement is relevant to [±human]

(95) hon -ko$_i$ iyu$^{?}$u -^{y}en -a -ko$_i$

child pl fall pst dec Ⅲpl

'Children fell down. '

(96) diri -ko$_i$ iyu$^{?}$u -^{y}en -a (-*ko$_i$)

stone pl fall pst dec Ⅲpl

'Stones fell down. '

(97) seta -ko$_i$ iyu$^{?}$u -^{y}en -a -ko$_i$

dog pl fall pst dec Ⅲpl

'Dogs fell down. '

The three examples above illustrate that if subject is [+animate] then subject agreement marker occurs while subject is [-animate] it cannot occur. In these cases, of course, subject agreement occurs to the right of the declarative marker *–a* due to no preverbal constituent. However in some cases subject agreement marker can occur immediately after the subject if a subject is [+human] as the following examples:

(98) ku^{w}a tan$_i$ –i$_i$ seno –len -a

boy Ⅲsg go pst.pef dec

'The boy had gone. '

(99) raam$_i$ –e$_i$ aandii -ken -a

Ram Ⅲsg marry pst dec

'Ram got married '

(100) soma$_i$ ondo somi$_j$ -kin$_{i+j}$ paiti -ken -a

Soma and Somi Ⅲdual work pst dec

'Soma and Somi worked. '

(101) hon –ko$_i$ –ko$_i$ gi -pi -l tan -a

child pl Ⅲpl fight1 VREC fight2 prog dec

'Children are fighting each other. '

There is no other constituent other than subject and verb in the above examples. So normally subject agreement marker occurs to the end of sentence. But here subject agreement markers come immediately after the subject when a subject is [+human].

In (102) and (103) there is no subject agreement marker after the negative *ka-*. If a subject is [+animate], the subject agreement marker must occur to the right of the negative in Ho

(102) diri -ko $_i$ ka -ø iyu$^{?}$u -^{y}en -a

stone pl neg fall pst dec

'Stones did not fall down. '

(103) am $_i$ kaji -keD -a ci am -a kiteb –ko $_j$ ka –ø bugin -a

you say pst dec comp you gen book pl neg good dec

'You said that your books are not good. '

In Ho the pronominal agreement marker can be used for the genitive in some cases where the head noun is [+human]. Here I will not cover other restrictions which will be discussed later.

(104) juRi -ñ = añ -a juRi

friend 1sg I gen friend

' my friend' 'my friend'

*(105) uri –ñ (56) añ -a uri

cow 1sg I gen cow

'my cow' 'my cow'

And there is another important role of the subject agreement marker in accordance with the [±animate] in a scrambling construction in Ho.

Agreement Hierarchy

Direct object and indirect object agreement marker cannot occur together in Ho. In other word only one of the two can occur to the verb as a suffix. So we may ask which agreement marker can occur when there is a direct object and an indirect object.

In Ho there is no pronominal strength hierarchy in agreement unlike Mizo and Hmar. Instead there seems to be a grammatical hierarchy in agreement among the subject, direct object and indirect object.

SUB Agr > IO Agr > DO Agr

(105a) pro $_i$ pro $_j$ ako -m $_i$ em -aD -iñ $_j$ -^{y}a

you me them IIsg give pst.pef I sg dec

SubAgr IO Agr

'You had given them to me.'

(105b) am $_i$ añ $_j$ ako -m $_i$ em -aD -iñ $_j$ -^{y}a

you me them IIsg give pst.pef I sg dec

'You had given them to me.'

As we have seen the order of DO and IO in the part 2, the unmarked sentence in Ho is Sub + IO + DO + V + Aux. The subject agreement marker must be shown in any sentences if subject is not [-animate]. Moreover the best position for Sub agreement is after preverbal constituent which is not dropped.

Thus if there is only subject and verb, Sub agreement occurs to the right of the declarative marker. And both direct and indirect object agreement marker cannot occur together. However indirect object agreement marker usually comes due to the strength of agreement as illustrated in (105).

Agreement and the lexical case marking

Direct object agreement marker cannot occur in the verb if the indirect object is not lexically case marked[22], but occurs in the verb if the indirect object is lexically case marked. However indirect object pronoun is also heavily dropped if it is not lexically case marked as illustrated in the following examples:

(82) pro $_i$ pro $_j$ mi^{y}ed' uli $_x$ –iñ $_i$ em– aD- mi $_j$ -^{y}a

I you one mango I sg give pst.pef IIsg dec

'I had given you a mango.'

---

[22] In Ho there is no accusative and dative marker as we have seen earlier.

In (105) and (82) the indirect objects are not lexically case marked. So its agreement marker must occur in the verb. Instead, the direct object agreement marker cannot come to the verb.

(106) pro $_i$ añ $_x$ –ta$^?$a kui-hon- ko $_j$ kul –keD– ko $_j$ -^{w}a– ben $_i$
you.polite me near girl pl send pst Ⅲpl dec Ⅱdual
'You sent girls to me. '

As mentioned ealier, if an indirect object is not lexically case marked, a direct object agreement marker must occur in the verb. The indirect object is lexically cased marked by the postposition *–ta$^?$a* 'near'.

So instead of the occurrence of the IO Agr marker, the 3rd plural direct object agreement marker *–ko* comes to the verb. But we should remember that a direct object cannot be lexically case marked due to the absence of accusative marker.

We can also find other examples from **non-nominative subject construction**. Ho language has a locative subject construction for physiological and mental ailments and possession. This subject is lexically case marked by a postposition *-ta?a -re* 'near to'. In Ho the NP which is lexically case marked does not show its agreement marker to the verb or the preverbal constituent.

(107) añ -ta$^?$a -re hasu –ø min -a (*-ñ)
I near to fever is dec
'I have a fever '

(108) añ -ta$^?$a -re gel taka (*-ñ) min -a (*-ñ)
I near to ten rupee is dec
'I have ten rupees '

Perhaps the examples above cannot be a Non-Nominative Subject if second constituent *hasu* 'fever' and *gel taka* ' ten rupee' are subject respectively.

However there seems to be exception in causative construction. Though the NP which is lexically case marked can bear agreement marker. But we may explain that exception case by thematic relations.

Agreement in causative constructions

In causative construction causative markers always occur to the right of the verb root. We already observed that the NP can not bear its agreement marker if the NP is lexically marked. e.g. when an indirect object is lexically case marked that agreement marker cannot appear, and in the locative subject construction subject agreement marker cannot occur. However we may find that oblique object also give its agreement marker occurs in causative construction.

(109)

$raam_i$	hon	ko_j	($ta^?a$)	ete	a^ye	$-^?a$	paiti	$-i_i$	paiti	-ici	$-ko_j$	$-^wa$
Ram	*child*	*pl*	*near*	*by*	*his*	*gen*	*work*	*IIIsg*	*work*	*Cau*	*IIIpl*	*dec*

'Ram will cause children to do his work.'

In (109) *hon-ko* 'children' is neither an indirect object nor a direct object. It is oblique object in Ho. However its agreement marker comes after causative marker. Let us assume that *hon-ko* functions as Agent due to thematic relationship. Though so, normally it cannot occur because it is lexically case marked. If so, how can we explain that problem? Is an oblique object stronger than other object? Is it true that it is an oblique object ?

But in examples below we find different case from (110). Though that is an oblique object it is not stronger than direct object in (110) and (111).

(110)	pro_i	$a^ye^?$	$-ta^?a$	-te	$-\tilde{n}_i$	pro_x	raa	-iri	$-me_x$	-tan	-a
	I	*him*	*near*	*by*	*Isg*	*you*	*cry*	*Cau*	*IIsg*	*pres*	*dec*

'I cause him to make you to cry. '

(111)	pro_i	$a^ye^?{}_j$	$-ta^?a$	-te	$-\tilde{n}_i$	pro_x	raa	-iri	-keD	$-me_x$	-a
	I	*him*	*near*	*By*	*Isg*	*you*	*cry*	*Cau*	*pst*	*IIsg*	*dec*

'I caused him to make you to cry.'

The causative construction in Ho needs only one verb carrying a causative marker to assign the theta-roles to all NPs regarding to essential agrument whereas in English it requires at least two verbs which can give the theta roles to all NPs in causative constructions. Thus we may reinterpret as the following:

Verb + *iri / ici*   :   < Instigator, Agent, Recipient, Patient> in Ho

From (110) we say that *añ* 'I' is an Instigator, $a^{y}e$ 'him' is an Agent and pro_x 'you' is a Patient. In Ho there is only one verb in causative construction while there are more than one verb in English.

Thus if our assumption is valid, we may account for that agreement case in terms of thematic role. The oblique object which is lexically case marked functions like an agent as shown in (109).

Thus even though it is lexically case marked its thematic role is stronger than the Theme which is a direct object. But in (110) and (111) even though $a^{y}e$ 'him' is an Agent it cannot give its agreement markers since there is another Agent *pro* 'you' which is nearer to the verb than farther Agent to the verb[23]. In other word, *pro* 'you' is the Agent of the verb *raa* 'cry' since 'you' delivers the action of 'cry' in the causative construction.

(112)

raam	ako_i	ta$^{?}$a	te	mohan	nikul	-ko	kule	-ici	-a	$-ko_i$	-^{w}a
Ram	*them*	*near*	*by*	*Mohan*	*letter*	*IIIpl*	*send*	*Cau*	*tense*	*IIIpl*	*dec*

'Ram caused them to s end letter to Mohan'

In (112) we clearly see thematic relationship regarding to agreement. *raam* 'Ram' is an Instigator, *ako* 'them' is an Agent, *mohan* 'Mohan' is a Recipient and *ciTTii* 'letter' is a Theme in (112). This relationship indicates that *ako* 'them' which is lexically case marked can bear its agreement inside verb while *mohan* 'Mohan' cannot though it is a Recipient. Because Agent is stronger than Recipient. And in Ho apart from the subject that is Instigator in causative construction only one agreement marker can occur inside verb.

Thus in (109) where Agent is stronger than Theme, the agreement marker is co-indexed with the Agent. And in (111) where nearer Agent (Agent 1) is stronger than farther Agent (Agent 2), the agreement is identical with the nearer Agent. Finally in

---

23 The concept of 'nearer' and 'farther' is borrowed from Minimal Link Condition (MLC)

(112) Agent gives its agreement marker inside verb.

To sum up, there is a thematic hierarchy in agreement as shown in below.

Agent > Recipient/Goal > Patient > Theme[24]

Though the NP is lexically case marked, it can give its agreement marker in causative construction in terms of thematic relationship.

After verb incorporation, [-transitive] verb may function as [+transitive] verb. Because Incorporation has a '*transitivizing effect*'. This phenomenon is also found in Ho. The verb *uTu* 'stand' and *giti* 'sleep' are intransitive verb. But they accompany with [+tr] marker *-D* .

(113)	meri	sohan	ta[?]a	-ete	(añ)$_i$	uTe	-ici	-ke	-D	-iñ $_i$	-a
	Mary	*Sohan*	*near*	*by*	*me*	*stand**[-tr]***	*Cau*	*pst*	***[+tr]***	*I sg*	*dec*

'Mary made Sohan to make me to stand up.'

(114)	mohan $_i$	raam	ta[?]a	-ete	hon $_j$	-e $_i$	giti	-ici	-ki	-e
	Mohan	*Ram*	*near*	*by*	*child*	*IIIsg*	*sleep**[-tr]***	*Cau*	*pst+**[+tr]***	*IIIsg* $_j$*+dec*

'Mohan made Ram to make child to sleep.'

Thus though verb is an intransitive it shows the object agreement marker after verb incorporation.

Long Distance Agreement

It is unclear that Ho language has long distance agreement. However the following sentence shows the case of long distance agreement.

---

[24] The reason why Patient is stronger than Theme is that [-animate] is weaker than [+animate] in Ho.

(115)

am$_i$	[añ$_j$	concoR]	-em$_i$	manatiŋ	-t	-aD	-iñ$_j$	-a
you	*me*	*intelligent*	*Ⅱsg*	*consider*	***t**-insertion*[25]	*pst.pef*	*Ⅰsg*	*dec*

'You considered me intelligent'

Under ECM *añ* 'me' is an Accusative Case though it is also subject of small clause. Thus its agreement marker *iñ* occurs to the right of the tense marker. In fact if it is to be a clear example of long distance agreement then its agreement marker must occur to the right of the declarative marker as in usual cases. Moreover the following sentences show ECM as well as subject of the small clause at the same time if the data is correct.

(116)

añ$_i$	[ini	-$^{?}$i$_j$	muuruku]	mana	-tiy	-tai	-i	-^{y}a
I	*him*	*Ⅲsg*	*stupid*	*consider*	*to*		*Ⅲsg*	*dec*

' I considered him stupid'

(117)	añ$_i$	[ini$_j$	-$^{?}$i$_j$	concoR]	-eñ$_i$	mana	tiy	tai	ø	-^{y}a
	I	*him*	*Ⅲsg*	*intelligent*	*Ⅰsg*	*consider*				*Dec*

' I considered him stupid'

Sentence (116) shows that *ini* 'him' functions as a subject of small clause and a direct object of a matrix clause at the same time in terms of the occurrence of the agreement marker *–i* 'Ⅲsg'. That is to say, the occurrence of the right of *ini* indicates that *ini* is a subject of small clause because only subject agreement marker can occur immediately after subject. And also it occurs to the direct object agreement position at the same time. Thus we may think that this case can illustrate how an Accusative Case under ECM can be a Subject of embedded clause. Sentence (117) illustrates that *ini* is not an object but a subject.

However the following shows that there is no long distance agreement in Ho since the subject of embedded clause does not have its agreement marker anywhere.

---

[25] In some cases t-insertion is founded in Ho such as suku**t** 'like' etct.

(118) pro$_i$ [am en-ta$^?$a seno ti^{y}a]-ñ$_i$ sanaŋ -tan -a

I you there go to I sg want pres dec

'I want you to go there '

(119) pro$_i$ aRsi -re nel –e -n ti^{y}a -am$_i$ sanaŋ -tan -a

you mirror in see epen VR to IIsg want pres dec

'You want to see yourself in the mirror '

Agreement in infinitive clauses

In Ho the root of the verb + *-ti^{y}a / -laged' / -te* forms infinitive clauses.

(120)a. pro$_i$ dilli seno -ti^{y}a -ø sanaŋ -tan -a -ñ$_i$

I Delhi go for want pres dec I sg

'I want to go to Delhi '

(120)b. pro$_i$ dilli seno -ti^{y}a -ñ sanaŋ -tan -a -ø

I Delhi go for I sg want pres dec

'I want to go to Delhi '

As we already observed earlier the subject agreement marker can occur only one time to the either of preverbal position or end of the sentence as again illustrated in (120) and (121). Somehow there seems to be an exception in ECM cases.

(121)a. raam$_j$ ondo sita$_i$ mandi -ø jom -ti^{y}a -ø sanaŋ -tan -a -kin$_{i+j}$

Ram and Sita rice eat for want pres dec IIIdual

'Ram and Sita want to eat rice '

(121)b. raam$_j$ ondo sita$_i$ mandi -ø jom -ti^{y}a -kin$_{i+j}$ sanaŋ -tan -a

Ram and Sita rice eat for IIIdual want pres dec

'Ram and Sita want to eat rice '

The following examples from (122) to (125) show that subject agreement marker cannot occur in infinitive clauses. Instead it occurs to the right of the preverbal constituent (infinitive clause). So in these cases PRO cannot give its agreement marker to any preverbal word of the infinitive clause.

(122)	pro$_i$	pro$_j$	en	puti	em	-am$_j$	-ti^{y}a	-ãñ$_i$	sanaŋ	-tan	-a
	I	*you*	*that*	*book*	*give*	*IIsg*	*To*	*I sg*	*want*	*pres*	*dec*

'I want to give that book to you '

(123)	raam$_i$	ondo	siita$_j$	puti	paRaaw	-lagid'	mundo	-kin$_{i+j}$	seno	-^{y}an	-a
	Ram	*and*	*Sita*	*book*	*read*	*for*	*school*	*IIIdual*	*go*	*pst*	*dec*

'Ram and Sita went to school to read book '

(124)	raam$_i$	ondo	siita$_j$	pro$_x$	nel	-am$_x$	-te	-kin$_{i+j}$	seno	-^{y}an	-a
	Ram	*and*	*Sita*	*you*	*see*	*IIsg*	*to*	*IIIdual*	*go*	*pst*	*dec*

'Ram and Sita went to see you '

(125)	pro$_i$	pro$_j$	kuihon	-ko	em	-am$_j$	-ti^{y}a	-ko$_i$	sanaŋ	-tan	-a
	they	*you*	*girl*	*IIIpl*	*give*	*you*	*to*	*IIIpl*	*want*	*pres*	*dec*

'They want to give girls to you '

Thus it can be illustrated as the following inventory:

Sub$_i$ [PRO$_i$ any word+(*Sub Agr$_i$) Verb+infinitive mrk]+Sub Agr$_i$ Verb + Tense mrk + dec

However the direct object agreement marker can occur between infinitive verb and infinitive marker as shown in (122) and (125).

(126)	ãñ	soma$_i$	owa$^?$	bai	-re	dengga	-ki	-i$^?$$_i$	-e
	I	*Soma*	*house*	*build*	*to*	*help*	*pst*	*IIIsg*	*dec*

' I helped Soma to build a house '

In (126) we cannot find that PRO of the infinitive clause gives its agreement marker inside infinitive clause though matrix subject and embedded clause are different.

Agreement in complementizer clauses

(127)

pro$_i$ kaji keD a ci añ$_j$ em$_i$ nel leD iñ$_j$ ^{y}a m$_i$

you say pst comp me Ⅱsg see pst. Ⅰsg dec Ⅱ

'You said that you had seen me '

(128)

pro$_i$ kaji -keD -a ci pro$_i$ pro$_j$ poisa -m$_j$ em -aD -iñ$_j$ -a

you say pst dec comp you me money Ⅱsg give pst.pef Ⅰsg dec

'You told that you had given me money.'

In (127) and (128) we find that subject is dropped in matrix clause as well as embedded clause due to the rich agreement. Anyway the subject agreement marker occurs only inside embedded clause unlike the case of infinitive clause.

Possessive Agreement

There seems to be no possessive agreement in Ho as the following examples:

(129) pro$_i$ am$_j$ -a ote -ko$_x$ -ñ nel -aD -ø -a

I you gen field pl Ⅰsg see pst.pef dec

'I had seen your fields '

(130) pro$_i$ a^{y}e$_j$ -a$^?$ gel juRi -ko$_x$ -ñ$_i$ nel -aD -ko$_x$ -^{w}a

I he gen ten friend pl Ⅰsg see pst.pef Ⅲpl dec

'I saw his ten friends '

In (129) there is no agreement inside verb. Because the object is [-animate] and tense is [+past]. And *–ko* 'Ⅲpl' agrees not with governor but with the head noun *gel uRi ko* 'ten friends' in (130).

However there is a sort of possessive agreement in other sentences as the following examples:

(131) jema$_i$ a^{y}e$_i$–$^?$a ote ria da$^?$a$_y$ soma$_j$ -a$^?$ ote -ko$_x$ –^{w}e$_i$ em -aD -i$_j$ -^{y}e

Jema he gen field gen water Soma gen field pl IIIsg give pst.pef IIIsg dec

'Jema had given her field's water to Soma's field '

(132) jema$_i$ a^{y}e –$^?$a ote ria da$^?$a añ$_j$ -a ote$_x$ –^{w}e$_i$ em -aD -iñ$_j$ -^{y}a

Jema he gen field gen water me gen field IIIsg give pst.pef I sg dec

'Jema had given his field's water to my field '

(133) jema$_i$ a^{y}e –$^?$a ote ria da$^?$a am$_j$ -a ote$_x$ –^{w}e$_i$ em -aD -mi$_j$ -^{y}a

Jema he gen field gen water you gen field IIIsg give pst.pef IIsg dec

'Jema had given his field's water to your field '

If so, how is it permissible? Because there is no possessive agreement in (129) and (130). We may think that 'water' is given to the possessor of the field where the head noun is [-animate] in (131), (132) and (133). Thus governing noun can bear agreement.

Agreement in conjunctive participle clauses

(134) pro$_i$ [PRO$_i$ huju -len -ete] [PRO$_i$ dub -ken -ete] jom -keD -a -ñ$_i$

I I come pst comp I sit pst comp eat pst dec Isg

'Having come and having sat, I ate '

(135)nen-ta$^?$a gel kui-hon-ko$_i$ [PRO$_i$ huju-len-ete][PRO$_i$ giti -ken-ete] puti-ko$_i$ paRaaw-keD-a

here 10 girl pl come pst cp sleep pst cp book IIIpl read pst dec

'Having come and having slept, ten girls read a book here '

The conjunctive participle *–ete/-te* occurs after the tense marker and declarative marker *–a* is dropped in subordinate clause. And in conjunctive participle clauses subject agreement marker cannot occur as shown in:

(136) bar kuitan-kin$_i$ [PRO$_i$ manDi(-*kin)$_i$ jom-keD -ete] puti -kin$_i$ paRaaw -keD -a

2 girl dual rice IIIdual eat pst cp book IIIdual read pst dec

'Two girls ate rice and then read a book '

(137) [PRO$_i$ haato sen -ken -ete] [PRO$_i$ puti –ø kiriŋ -leD -ete] pro$_i$ huju ure –a –ñ $_i$

village go pst cp book buy pst cp come back dec I sg

'Having gone to the village and having bought a book, I will come back '

As we can see from the above examples though there is other constituent other than verb, preverbal word, subject agreement marker does not appear. And also subject agreement marker does not occur after negative in subordinate clause as shown in:

(138) [PRO$_i$ mundo ka -ø sen -ken -ete] borjo $_i$ a^{y}e -a$^?$ juRi owa$^?$ seno -^{y}an -a

school not go pst cp Borjo he gen friend house go pst dec

'Not having gone to the school Borjo went to his friend's house '

However direct object and indirect object agreement markers occur in the verb unlike while subject agreement marker does not occur since subject agreement marker can occur only one time. The position of IO or DO agreement is the same place where IO or DO agreement does in declarative sentence.

(139a) pro $_i$ [PRO$_i$ kuihon-ko $_j$ (*-ñ)$_i$ nel -keD –ko $_j$ -ete] jom -keD -a -ñ $_i$

I girl pl see pst Ⅲpl cp eat pst dec Isg

'I saw girls and then I ate '

(139b) pro$_i$ [PRO$_i$ kuihon-ko $_j$ (*-ñ)$_i$ seta em -aD –ko $_j$ -ete] seno -^{y}an -a -ñ $_i$

I girl pl dog give pst Ⅲpl cp eat pst dec Isg

'I gave a dog to the girls and then I went '

(140) pro$_i$ PRO$_j$ huju -tan -iñ$_j$ nel -ki$^?$ –i$_i$ -^{y}a

I he come-prog –1sg see –pst –3sg -dec

'I saw him coming.'

In the sentence (140) the subject agreement marker occrrs to the right of the small clause since the clause is regarded as a preverbal constituent. Moreover the subject of the small clause which is a direct object of the matrix clause is shown to the verb as a direct oject agreement marker.

Agreement in relative clauses

(141) en kui-hon-ko$_i$ okon -ko hola –ñ beta -leD -ko -a añ -a juRi -ko
that girl pl whom Ⅲpl Y.day Isg meet pst Ⅲpl dec I gen friend pl
'Those girls whom I met yesterday are my friends '

(142) en sepeD$_i$ okun puti -i $_i$ paRaaw -tan -a (ini)$_i$ esu murkuu -e
that boy who book Ⅲsg read prog dec very stupid dec+Ⅲsg $_i$
'That boy who is reading a book is very stupid '

In (141) the subject agreement marker occurs in preverbal position and head noun *en kui-hon-ko* ' those girls' which is a direct object still shows its agreement marker inside relative clause. And in the present tense verb 'be' is strongly dropped in Ho.

Thus (141) can be reinterpreted as the following inventory:

[Head Noun(DO)$_i$ [Relative Pronoun$_i$ pro$_j$ adverb+Sub Agr$_j$ Verb+DO Agr$_i$]] VP

In (142) the head noun which is identical with relative pronoun also shows its subject agreement marker in embedded clause as well as in matrix clause. And the matrix subject agreement marker also can be suffixed after free relative pronouns.

(143) jai $_i$ –re –^{y}o johar opis–re huju -^{w}e -(ina), pro$_j$ sukut -i$^?$$_i$ -^{y}eñ $_j$
anyone emph Johar office to come dec+Ⅲsg dubi I like Ⅲsg dec + Isg
'Whoever comes to Johar office, I like '

(143) pro $_i$ jai $_j$ -m $_i$ sukut -i $_j$ –e –(ina), añ $_x$ -^{y}o -ñ $_x$ sukut –i $_j$ -e
you anyone Ⅱsg like Ⅲsg dec dubi I emph I sg like Ⅲsg dec
'Whomever you like, I also like '

In (1*44*) and (145) each free relative pronoun also has its agreement marker since they function as a subject and a direct object, respectively.

(144) hon –ko$_i$ jana$_j$ -ko$_i$ jom -e $_j$ -^{y}a –(ina) añ $_x$ - ^{y}o -ñ $_x$ jom -e$_j$ -^{y}a
children anything Ⅲpl eat Ⅲsg dec dubi I emph I sg eat Ⅲsg dec
'Whatever children eat, I also eat '

(145) pro $_i$ jaacimi -te -m $_i$ seno -a -(ina) añ -^{y}o -ñ seno -a

you anytime Ⅱsg go dec dubi I emph I sg go dec

'Whenever you go, I also go '

(146) pro $_i$ jaapam -te -m $_i$ seno -a -(ina) añ -^{y}o -ñ seno -a

you anywhere e Ⅱsg go dec dubi I emph I sg go dec

'Wherever you go, I also go '

However free relative pronouns which do not function as either subject or direct object or indirect object cannot have their agreement as shown in (145) and (146).

From the above examples we may find the regularity of the form of free relatives, that is to say, *ja(jaa)* + noun as shown in :

ja + i 'whoever'
any Ⅲsg

ja + na 'whatever'
any thing

jaa + cimi 'whenever'
any time

jaa + pam 'wherever'
any place

If so, then we may find one interesting thing in the form of free relatives. Instead of suffixing 3rd pronoun to form 'whoever' and 'whomever', they just put the Ⅲ sg agreement marker. And, of course, there is Ⅲsg agreement . Thus we may think that this Ⅲsg agreement marker can be an indefinite marker[26] in Ho.

Participial clauses also show agreement case as like participle construction as the following examples:

(147) [a^{y}e$^?$ sabii -ø kula $_i$] añ -ta$^?$a –te agu –i $_i$ -pe

he catch fut tiger me near to bring Ⅲsg imperative

'Bring to me the tiger which you will catch '

[26] In interrogative pronouns we also find that *okoe* 'who' can be broken into *oko* + *e* 'Ⅲsg Agr', and also *okona* 'which thing' can be broken into *oko* + *na* 'thing'.

(148) pro $_i$ pro $_j$ [a^{y}e$^?$ pro $_i$ em -aD -iñ $_i$ laD] –eñ $_i$ em -a -me $_j$ -^{y}a
I you he me give pst.pef I sg bread I sg give epen IIsg dec
'I will give to you the bread which he had given to me '

Sentence (148) indicates that Ho is a very heavy pro-drop language due to agreement.

Agreement in anaphoric sentences

Recall that in Ho there must be an agreement marker of DO or IO as a suffix if IO and DO are [+animate] in transitive sentences. But we cannot find those agreement markers in anaphoric sentences.

Let us have a look at the following examples:

(149) pro $_i$ añ -te -ge -ñ $_i$ goe$^?$ -ke -n -a
I me I sg kill pst [-tr] dec
'I killed myself '

(150) añ añ -ge nikul ool -la -D -iñ -^{y}a
I me emph letter write pst.pef [Tr] 1sg dec
'I had written a letter to myself

(151) pro $_i$ aRsi -re -m $_i$ nel -ke -n -a
you mirror in IIsg see pst VR dec
'You saw yourself in the mirror'

(152) pro $_i$ añ -te -ge –ñ $_i$ toke -kie -n -a
I me by emph I sg hit pst VR dec
'I hit mysef '

If we know that an intransitive marker is *–n* in Ho, then we may know that *–n* can be a detransitivizer. So due to this reason there is no DO and IO Agreement marker. That is to say, the transitive verb is detransitivized in an anaphoric sentence. Thus the

DO agreement and IO agreement cannot occur in anaphoric sentences. Though there is *an-te-ge* 'me' for emphatic its agreement marker cannot occur.

We can not find that verbal reflexive also function as indirect object without any nominal reflexive. Thus, pronoun nominal occurs to the indirect object position and the indirect object agreement marker must occur to the verb as an infix.And there is also no Agr in the reciprocal sentences. Because *–n* still plays a role as a detransitivizer as the following examples:

(153) ale$_i$	ce	-pe	–reb	-ke	**-n**	-a	-le$_i$
we	*V1*	*VREC*	*V2*	*pst*	*[-tr]*	*dec*	*I pl*

'We kissed each other '

(154) alaŋ	ne	-pe	-l	-aka	-n	-a
we.dual	*V1*	*VREC*	*V2*	*pres.prf*	*[-tr]*	*dec*

'We, two have seen each other '

However subject agreement marker occurs after infinitive clause. Because that infinitive clause itself is preverbal constituent as a complement as the following example:

(155)	pro$_i$	aRsi	-re	nel	-e	-n	-ti^{y}a	-ñ	sanaŋ	-tan-a
	I	*mirror*	*in*	*see*	*epen*	*[-tr]*	*to*	*I sg*	*want*	*pres dec*

'I want to see myself in the mirror '

(156)		aRsi	-re	nel	-e	-n	ti^{y}a	-m	sanaŋ	-leD	-a
	you	*mirror*	*in*	*see*	*epen*	*[-tr]*	*to*	*IIsg*	*want*	*pst.pef*	*dec*

'You wanted to see yourself in the mirror '

Verbal reflexive *–n* does not affect to main verb *sanaŋ* 'want' as a detransitivizer. If so, can DO agreement occur in sentence such as 'I wanted him to see himself in the mirror'? Due to the shortage of data we may not answer to that. But logically DO agreement for 'him' cannot occur in main verb because infinitival clause is a complement so that it functions as a DO.

Agreement as a genitive

In Ho a pronominal agreement marker functions as a possessive marker in some cases. There is, of course, a distinctive possessive marker as we have seen in part 2. Let us have a look at the following examples:

(157) añ -a apu = apu -ñ
I gen father *father I sg*
'my father' 'my father'

(158) am -a apu = apu -m
you gen father *father IIsg*
'your father' 'your father'

However, the pronominal agreement marker is not used for a genitive all the time. There is a restriction that the relation between a head and its governing noun must be [+humanbeing] and that 3rd person pronominal agreement marker cannot function like that way as we already observed in part 2.

(159) juRi -ñ = añ -a juRi
friend I sg *I gen friend*
' my friend' 'my friend'

*(160) uri –ñ ⇒ añ -a uri
cow I sg *I gen cow*
'my cow'

And we also find the direction of governing of head noun in some cases. That is from right to left as in SVO language.

Agreement and scrambling

Ho is a verb final language. The subject precedes the object in unmarked sentence. And the subject agreement marker must occur to the object which is located in preverbal position if the subject is [+animate]. But there is no rule that the subject should be expressed before the object in Ho. Thus scrambling is permissible in Ho. When the object precedes the subject the subject agreement marker cannot occur to the any position.

Let us have a look at the following examples:

(161) kuihon -ko $_i$ raam $_j$ -ko $_i$ tam –ki$^{?}$ -i $_j$ -^{y}e

girl pl Ram Ⅲpl hit pst Ⅲsg dec

Subject Object

'The girls hit Ram '

(162) raam $_j$ -ø kuihon-ko $_i$ tam -ki$^{?}$ -i $_j$ -^{y}a

Ram girl pl hit pst Ⅲsg dec

Object Subject

'The girls hit Ram '

*(163) raam $_j$ -ko$_i$ kuihon-ko $_i$ tam -ki$^{?}$ -i $_j$ -^{y}a

Ram Ⅲpl girl pl hit pst Ⅲsg dec

Object Subject

'The girls hit Ram '

(164) raam $_i$ sita $_j$ -e $_i$ tam -ki$^{?}$ -i $_j$ -^{y}a

Ram Sita Ⅲsg hit pst Ⅲsg dec

Subject DO

'Ram hit Sita'

(165) sita $_j$ -ø raam $_i$ tam -ki$^{?}$ -i $_j$ -^{y}a

Sita Ram hit pst Ⅲsg dec

DO Subject

'Ram hit Sita '

*(166) sita $_j$ -e $_i$ raam $_i$ tam -ki$^{?}$ -i $_j$ -^{y}a

Sita Ⅲsg Ram hit pst Ⅲsg dec

'Ram hit Sita '

In (162) and (165) we can see that there is no subject agreement marker when there is a scrambling, namely the object precedes the subject. This means that a subject agreement marker should not be shown when there is a scrambling between the subject and the object which are both referential expressions as well as [+animate].

In (102) and (104) there is no subject Agreement marker respectively. The subject agreement marker *–ko* cannot occur to the object *raam* as well as to the right of the declarative marker *–ʸa* as in (163) and the subject agreement marker *–e* also cannot come to the right of *sita* as well as *-ʸa* as in (166).

In other way, we may say that the scrambling of the subject and the object does not allow to show the subject agreement marker. Of course, though there is still a direct object agreement marker.

However, the subject agreement marker comes when the subject and object are [±animate] respectively. Let us consider the following examples:

(167) raam $_i$ kadal -ko –e $_i$ kiriŋ -keD -a

Ram banana pl IIIsg buy pst dec

'Ram bought bananas '

(168) kadal -ko raam $_i$ -e $_i$ kiriŋ -keD -a

banana pl Ram IIIsg buy pst dec

'Ram bought bananas '

In (167) and (168) we can also see the role of [±animate] or thematic relationship in Ho.

(169) kuihon-ko $_i$ hola -ko $_i$ seno -yen -a

girl pl yesterday IIIpl go pst.pef dec

'The girls had gone yesterday '

(170) hola -ko $_i$ kuihon -ko $_i$ seno –yen -a

yesterday IIIpl girl pl go pst.pef dec

'Yesterday the girls went '

Sentences (169) and (170) show that there is no problem for scrambling regarding to subject agreement between subject and other constituent. Only relation between subject and direct object bears limitation regarding to subject agreement.

Now we may wonder why the subject agreement marker cannot occur to the any position when there is a scrambling between the [+animate] subject and the [+animate] object. The reason is that the subject agreement marker can also occur to the right of the subject itself in some cases. Let us have a look at the following examples:

(171) raam $_i$ –e $_i$ aandii -ken -a

Ram IIIsg marry pst dec

'Ram got married '

(172) soma $_i$ ondo somi $_j$ -kin $_{i+j}$ paiti -ken -a

Soma and Somi IIIdual work pst dec

'Soma and Somi worked '

(173) hon –ko $_i$ –ko $_i$ gi -pi -l tan -a

child pl IIIpl fight1 VREC fight2 prog dec

'Children are fighting each other '

Let us say that the reason of the absence of subject agreement marker in such types of scrambling is to avoid the confusion between Agent and Patient in Ho. So the solution can be in terms of the thematic relationship[27]. If this is true, this also indicates that the AGR may relate to the thematic role. Thus subject agreement marker can occur after direct object when there is scrambling between Agent and Theme in (173).

Agreement and negation

(174) pro $_i$ gapa en –ta'a ka *(-e') $_i$ seno –ø - a

he tomorrow there neg IIIsg go fut dec

' He will not go there tomorrow '

[27] However this solution is very abstract. I admit that I could not figure out properly due to the short of the data.

(175) ako $_i$ musiŋ - musiŋ ka -ko $_i$ unuŋ -tan -a

they day day neg Ⅲpl play pres dec

' Not often they play '

In Ho if the subject is a [+animate] then the subject agreement marker must occur to the right of the negative in a negative sentence. The negative is always located in a preverbal position. But if the subject is [-animate] then only the negative *ka-* occurs to the preverbal position without subject agreement marker.

(176) ciken reya ka –a$^?$ -ge ?

why not dec emph

'Why not? '

(177) a^{y}e$^?$ uRu -tan -a ci [pro $_i$ jaai -re-^{y}o ka –e $_i$ aDaan -a]

he think pres dec comp anyone emph neg Ⅲsg know dec

'He think that he dose not know anyone '

(178) a^{y}e$^?$ $_i$ ka -e$^?$ $_i$ uRu -tan -a ci [pro $_i$ jaai -re-^{y}o aDaan -a]

he neg Ⅲsg think pres dec comp anyone emph know dec

'He does not think that he knows anyone '

In (177) there is a subject agreement marker *–e* after the negative in embedded clause even though the subject is dropped.

(178) pro $_i$ nen -em $_i$ sanaŋ -tan -a ci ka -ø $_{*i}$

you this Ⅱsg like pres dec or neg

'You like this or not ? '

(179) añ $_i$ uRu -tan -a ci ka –e $_{*i}$ gama -ø -^{y}a

I think pres dec comp not Ⅲsg rain fut dec

'I think that it will rain '

In (179) there is no subject in embedded clause. But the subject agreement marker *–e* comes. How is it possible? We may guess that the nature phenomenon can be considered as [+animate] in Ho.

And there is another form of negative marker in an imperative sentence. And 2nd person agreement marker must occur to that negative instead of occurring to the end of the sentence as the following examples:

(180) nen	ta$^{?}$a	-re	alo	-m	seno	-^{w}a
	there	*in*	*donot*	*IIsg*	*go*	*dec*

'Do not go there ' - to one person

(181)	pro$_{i}$	alo	-pe	tam	-iñ$_{i}$	-a
	me	*donot*	*IIpl*	*hit*	*I sg*	*dec*

'Do not hit me ' -to many person

(182)	pro$_{i}$	mi^{y}ed	puti	alo	-ben	em	-a	-ko$_{i}$	-^{w}a
	to them	*one*	*book*	*donot*	*IIdual*	*give*	*epen*	*IIIpl*	*dec*

'Do not give a book to them ' -to two person or polite form

(183)	pro$_{i}$	mi^{y}ed	puti	em	-a	-ko	-ben
	to them	*one*	*book*	*give*	*epen*	*IIIpl*	*IIdual*

'Give a book to them(dual) '

While the subject agreement marker occurs to the end of the sentence in the positive imperative sentence, the subject agreement marker comes to the right of the negative marker *alo-*.

And when the verb 'be' comes as a verb in the negative sentence, no subject agreement can occur to the negative as the following example:

(184)	en	sepeD	raja	ka	-ø	(tan	-a	-e)	=	en	sepeD	raja	ka
	that	*boy*	*king*	*not*	*is*		*dec*	*IIIsg*					

'That boy is not a king '

Agreement in Null-Dative Subject Constructions

Though there is no dative case marker in Ho it has a dative subject apart from the locative subject construction. Namely, that is Null-Dative-Subject Construction.

According to L.Burrows(1980:86), it is argued that 'when conjugated impersonally, the pronominal sign denoting the person who experiences the physical or mental condition is inserted in the verb in the same way as the animate object-sigh of transitive verbs'. His statement indicates that the dative subject construction depends on the position of the occurrence of the subject agreement marker. In other word if the subject agreement marker occurs to the position of the direct object agreement marker, then it is a dative subject construction whereas if the subject agreement marker occurs to the end of the declarative marker in the same way as an intransitive verb construction.

Let us have a look at the following examples from L.Burrows[28] (1980:86):

(185) suku -iñ -tan[29] -a

please I sg pres dec

'It please me'

(186a) suku -ke -D -iñ -a

please pst [+tr] I sg dec

'It pleased me'

(186b) pro $_i$ suku -ea -n -a -ñ $_i$

I please pst [-tr] dec I sg

'I was pleased'

(186c) hasu -ñ -tan -a

pain I sg pres dec

'It pains me'

(186d) pro $_i$ hasu -tan -a -ñ $_i$

I pain pres dec I sg

'I am painful'

The examples above illustrated that impersonal verbs denoting physical feelings or mental conditions can have a dative construction though there is no dative case marker since the position of the subject agreement marker makes the distinction semantically between the dative subject construction and the intransitive verb construction in Ho. Thus we may say that Ho language has Null-Dative-Subject Construction on the basis of the position of the subject agreement marker.

---

[28] He defines that sentences (125.a) and (126.a) are Impersonal while (125.b) and (126.b) are Personal.

[29] It is unclear that *–tan* also functions as a verb 'be' in Ho. However I claim that only *–min* is a verb 'be'. Because *–min* can be occurred with both a noun and an adjective whereas *–tan* can be occurred with only a noun. And the past form of the verb 'be' is *tai* in Ho. Thus *taiken* can be broken into *tai* 'to stay or live' and *ke-n* 'intransitive past marker'. Moreover the form of the past continuous is *–tan taiken*. Hence *–tan* can be an aspect marker in Ho.

The rest part of Agreement

There is no agreement with the gender, article, demonstrative and number. And also there seems not to be default agreement. And dual agreement marker can be used for honorific expression in Ho as we have seen earlier in Part 2. And the agreement marker in some cases replaces the numeral as shown in:

(187)	bar	puti	=	puti	-kin
	two	*book*		*book*	*Ⅲdual*

' Two books'

According to J. Deeney(1966) a possessive from of the noun or pronoun is put before the noun denoting that which is owned, and the proper form of the verb 'be' is used for a non-nominative subject construction. However he says that there is an ambiguity as illustrated in:

(188)	añ	-a	hon	$-ko_i$	ban	$-ko_i$	$-^wa$
	I	*gen*	*child*	*Ⅲpl*	*is not*	*Ⅲpl*	*dec*

(a) 'I have no children.'

(b) 'My children are not here.'

However the example above cannot be ambiguous in terms of the position of the occurrence of the subject agreement. If that expression means b.interpretation, the subject agreement marker must occur to the right of the declartive marker *–a* since the subject agreement marker cannot occur to the left of the declarative marker in Ho. Thus in (a) interpretation, the subject is *añ* 'I' which is lexically case marked by the possessive marker and so that its agreement marker cannot occur to the end of sentence. Instead hon-ko 'children' shows its agreement marker in the direct object agreement position.

Hence logically the sentence which has (b) interpretation is illustrated as the following example:

(189)	añ	-a	hon	$-ko_i$	ban	$-^wa$	$-ko_i$
	I	*gen*	*child*	*Ⅲpl*	*is not*	*dec*	*Ⅲpl*

(b) 'My children are not here.'

Example from Santali and So:ra:

In Santali the subjet agreement marker is attached to the word that immediately precedes the verb, or occupies the final position in the verb form as like Ho, Mundari and So:ra:. And animate direct object are expressed by pronouns affixed to the verb as following:

(190) idi -me -a -e
take -2sg –FIN –3sg
'He will take you.'

(191) ere -keT -le -a -kin
deceive –pst –1pl –FIN –3dual
'They(two) decived us.'

(192) b'hu$_i$ -i$_i$ pro$_j$ gu -ked -e$_j$ -a
wife -3sg bring –pst-3sg-FIN
'He broght a wife.'

The pronominal suffixes referring either to the direct object or to the indirect object can not occur together as found in Ho. And in Santali possessor suffix appear to the verb. The concerned object function is expressed by the possessor suffix –ta or –t on the verb, preceding the pronominal suffix as followings:

(193a) pro$_i$ pro$_j$ dal -iñ$_j$ -a -e$_i$
he me strike –1sg -IND –3sg
'H ewill strike me.'

(193b) pro pro dal -t -iñ -a -e
he strike –poss-1sg-IND-3sg
'He will strike mine.

Moreover the concerned object pronominal (possessive agreement marker) can co-occur with the direct object pronominals as below:

(194) pro$_i$ pro$_j$ dal -e -t -iñ$_j$ -a -e$_i$
he me strike-3sg –poss-1sg –IND-3sg
'He will strike him who is mine.'

In So:ra: nouns as like personl pronouns are to be contracted when they are incorporated with other words. So the verb with its object forms one compound word as showin in (195).

(195) (anin) gij -iñ -te: -n

he see 1sg –pst-3sg

'He saw me.'

However, nouns which have contracted forms are also incorporated with the verb. This case is not found in Ho and Mundari. The contraction of a word is due to the loss of (a) initial, (b) the medial or (c) the final sound(s). In the following examples the noun *jo:* (the contracted form *ajo:-n* 'fish') and *pu*: (the contracted form *pu pu:-n* 'cake') is added directly to the root as *–iñ* the sentence (195).

(196) (anin) ŋam -jo: -te -n

he catch-fish-does-pres-3sg

'He is catching fish.'

(197) pro bal -pu: -te -ji

they bake -cake –pres –3pl

'They are baking a cake.'

As we observed the subject agreement marker also occurs to the end of the verb as like Ho, and Mundari and Santali. Interestingly a noun –obect and a pronominal object may be incorporated with a verb as following:

(198) pro paŋ -ti -dar -iŋ -te: -n

he bring -give -rice -1sg –pst -3sg

'He brought and gave me cooked rice .'

And two noun objects may be incorporated with the verb as following:

(199) ŋen po: -puŋ -kun -t -am

I stab -belly -knife -futrue-2ng

'I will stab your belly with a knife'

(200) ŋen aj -ja: -dar -si: -t -am

I not -receive -rice -hand –future-you

'I will not receive cooked rice from your hand.'

The sentences (199) and (200) show that the subject agreement marker can not occur to the end of the verb since the other pronominal suffix occurs to indicate the possessive relation with the second noun which is closer to the suffix. However no pronominal object is incorporated with the present-perfect participle as is a noun object.

21. Non-nominative subject construction

With psychological predicates or when the logical subject is a possessor, the subject (possessor or experiencer) carries dative or genitive or locative postposition. The verb in such cases agrees with the possessed noun phrases (theme or patient) (K.V. Subbarao). In Ho there seems to be Non-nominative subject constructions. However, this non-nominative subject construction is not common or could be influenced by Hindi. Let us consider the following examples:

(1) sema raãsaa (min -a)
Sema happy is dec
'Sema is happy. '

(2) pro$_i$ bo:o$^?$ hasu -ñ$_i$ tan -a
I head pain I sg is dec
'I have a headache. '

(3) añ -ta$^?$a -re hasu –ø min -a
I near to fever is dec
'I have a fever. '

(4) añ -ta$^?$a -re gel taka min -a
I near to ten rupee is dec
'I have ten rupees. '

In Ho they might use a locative subject construction for physiological and mental ailments and possession instead of the dative subject construction due to the absence of the dative case marker. According to J.Deeney there is also possessive subject construction.

22. Conjunctive participles

In this construction the sentence carries a finite verb and all the subordinate clauses carry a participial form of the verb which must be [+ past tense] and the declarative marker *–a* must be dropped.

Verb + past tense marker + (* declarative *–a*) + *ete / canam*   'Having - en '

(5)

pro_i	[pro_i	huju	-len	-ete]	[pro_i	dub	-ken	-ete]	jom	-keD	-a	-ñ $_i$
I	*I*	*come*	*pst*	*cpm*	*I*	*sit*	*pst*	*cpm*	*eat*	*pst*	*dec*	*I sg*

'Having come and having sat and I ate. '

(6)

pro_i	pro_i	huju	-len	-canam	pro_i	dub	-ken	-canam	jom	-keD	-a	-ñ $_i$
I	*I*	*come*	*pst*	*after*	*I*	*sit*	*pst*	*after*	*eat*	*pst*	*dec*	*I sg*

'Having come and having sat and I ate. '

(7) en   -canam / * en -ete

this   *after*

'after this'

While the conjunctive participle *–ete/-te* occurs only after the verb, the postposition *–canam* occurs after the verb as well as the noun. However when *–canam* is used as a conjunctive participle, the preceding verb must be also [+finite].

(8)

nenta$^{?}$a	gel kuihon ko $_i$[pro_i huju len ete]	[pro_i	giti	ken	ete] puti	ko paRaaw-keD-a
here	*10 girl pl* *come pst cpm*		*sleep*	*pst*	*cpm*	*book-3sg read –pst-dec*

'Having come and having slept and ten girls read a book. '

The conjunctive participle *–ete/-te* must occur with the past tense marker in Ho. And in subordinate clauses the subject agreement marker cannot occur[30]

---

[30] Even though there is a constituent such as an adverb, a direct object in the subordinate clause, no subject agreement marker comes to the preverbal position.

To study the structure of the conjunctive participles, the notion of verb + conjunctive participle is not sufficient. We need to have a holistic view of conjunctive participles (hereafter CP) to understand its structure. We need to see what it contains and how it behaves.

(9)	ini?	maanDi	jom-	ke-	D	ete	giti?	-ye-	n-	a -we
	he	food	eat	pst	[+tr]	cpm	sleep	pst	[-tr]	dec-3sg

'He ate food and slept'.

(10)	owa?	hujur-	ye-	n-	ete	hasda$_i$	uli-e$_i$	jom-e-a
	home	return	pst	[-tr]	cpm	Hasda	mango-3sg	eat-3sg-dec

'After returning home Hasad will eat a mango'.

In Ho, the conjunctive participial clause precedes the matrix verb.

(11)	oRaa	ke-	n-	ete	birui	maanDi –e	jom-ke-D-a
	bathe	pst	[-tr]	cpm	Biru	meal-3sg	eat-pst-[+tr]-dec

'Biru ate his meal after taking bath'.

(12)	Diyan	nu-	ke-	ete	raaju	giti?	ye - n -a-w-e$_i$
	rice beer	drink	pst	cpm	Raju	sleep	pst- [-tr] –decl-3sg

'Raju slept after drinking rice beer'.

In Ho, CP is [+tensed]. It also carries the [± transitive] marker according to its verb root. In Ho, the past marker is *ke-D* or *ke–n* where */D /* is the [+transitive] marker and /n/ is the [-transitive] marker.

(13)	ini?	puti-e	paRaaw	ke-	D-	a
	he	book-3sg	read	pst	[+tr]	decl

'He read a book'.

(14)	ini?	puti	paRaaw-	ke-	ete	inuŋ-	tan-	e
	he	book	read	Pst	cpm	play	prog	dec+3sg

'He is playing after reading a book'.

(15)	sabita	haaTo-e	seno-	ye-	n-	a
	Sabita	market-3sg	go	pst	[-tr]	decl

'Savita went to the market'.

(16)	sabita$_i$	haaTo	seno-	ye-	n-ete	uli	-ko -we$_i$	kiriŋ -ke –D	-a
	Savita	market	go	pst	[-tr] cpm	mango-pl-3sg		buy –pst –[+tr]-dec	

'Savita went to the market and bought mangoes'.

The various functions of CP in Ho

Sequential Actions (As a Conjunction)

(17)

PRO	haaTo	seno-	ye-	n-	ete	-puti	kiriŋ –ke –D	-ete	hujur	-a -ñ
	market	go	pst	[-tr]	cpm –book		buy –pst –[tr]	-cpm	come-dec-1sg	

'I will go to the market, buy a book and come back'.

(18)

borjo	mɛc	nel-	ke-	D-	ete	manDi	jom -keD –ete giti –yen –a -e
Borjo	match	see	pst	[+tr]	cpm	food	eat-pst -cpm sleep-pst-dec-3sg

'Borjo saw the match, had food and slept'.

(19)

am	oRaa	ke-	n-	ete	bongaa	KeD	ete	manDi –m	jom -keD –a	ci ?
you	bathe	pst	[-tr]	cpm	pray	pst	cpm	meal –2sg	eat-pst –dec ques	

'Do you eat after taking bath and saying the praying?'

Notice that in sentences (17) to (19) the CP works in denoting the sequential actions. The actions are done by the same subject. Also notice that, it is not necessary that the tense of the CP clause and the tense of the matrix clause should agree. The tense of the CP clause is always past whereas the tense of the matrix clause can be past or some other tense as in (17) and (19).

The fact that 'ete' imparts sequential interpretation clearly shows that 'ete' is not a non-finite causal construction

Conjunctive Participles as a Manner Adverb

(20)

hon nir- ke- n- ete mundo beTa -keD -e

child run pst [-tr] cpm school reach –pst -dec+3sg

'The child reached school running'.

(21)

ini$^?$ honaŋ boro- ke- n- ete buru -ria horaa-e parom –e tan a

he perhaps frighten pst [-tr] cpm forest –of path –3sg cross -epen-prog-dec

'He is crossing the path of the forest in fright'.

(22)

gita oyar- ke- n- ete bandaa –e parom keD –a

Gita swim pst [-tr] cpm pond -3sg cross pst -dec

'Gita has crossed the pond by swimming'.

(23)

sabin- ko bo?o sab ke (-D) -ete dub -taikin -a -ko

everybody head hold pst ([+tr]) cpm sit -pst.prog -dec -dec

'Everybody was siting holding their heads'.

Notice that in sentences (20) to (23) the CP works as a manner adverb. Again notice that the [± transitive] markers come according to the verbs and the tense of the CP clause does not agree with that of the matrix clause as in the sentences (20) to (23).

Conjunctive Participles as a Reason Adverb

(24) biru juDi lo?o napam ke- n- ete -rããsaa -ye -n -a

Viru friend comt meet pst [-tr] cpm -happy -pst -[-tr] -dec

'Viru felt happy meeting his friend'.

(25) PRO_i keDe nir- ke- n- ete $bimla_i$ -lagaa -yen -a $-e_i$

fast run pst [-tr] cpm bimla -tired -pst -dec -3sg

'Bimla was tired after running fast'.

(26) hasuten ho red jom -ke -D -ete suku -nam -keD -a

sick man medicine eat pst [+tr] cpm rest -get -pst dec

'The sick person got relief after taking the medicine'.

(27) phaThaakaa ria saaRi ayum -ke –D -ete hon-ko$_i$ boro -tan -a -ko$_i$

cracker of sound hear Pst [+tr] -cpm child-pl scrae –pres-dec-3sg

'Children get scared after hearing the sound of a cracker'.

(28) pure manDi Jom -ke- -D –ete aye -laai -re hasu yen -a

more food eat Pst [+tr] cpm his -stomach -in pain pst dec

'After eating too much he had a stomach ache'.

Notice that from (24) to (28), the conjunctive participle works as a reason adverb. The CP clause precedes the matrix verb.

The instead of Interpretation of Conjunctive Participles

(29) mundo ka -e seno- ye- n- ete borjo juRi owa$^{?}$ seno –yen -a

school neg -3sg go pst [+tr] cpm borjo friend house go –pst -dec

'Borjo went to his friend's place instead of going to the school'.

(30) ini$^{?}$ nogoDtia ka -$^{?}$e jom -ke -D -ete buluŋ$_j$ -te jom -e$_j$ -tan -a

he sweets neg 3sg eat pst [+tr] cpm snacks -by eat -3sg -prog -dec

'He is eating snacks instead of sweets'.

(31) gita ote- re ka –e giti$^{?}$–ke -n -ete plang -re giti$^{?}$ -yen -a

Gita floor on neg –3sg sleep pst [-tr] cpm bed on sleep –pst -dec

'Gita slept on the bed instead of sleeping on the floor'.

Notice that in (29) to (31) the conjunctive participle works in the instead of interpretation. The negation marker precedes conjunctive participle.

Lexical subjects as the subject of a CP cluse in Ho

It is interesting to find out that lexical subjects are permitted as the subjects of a CP clause in Ho, whereas in Hindi, Punjabi, Kashmiri they are not permitted as the subjects of a CP clause.

Hindi-Urdu (Indo-Ayran)

(32) *	kursi	TuT-	kar	bacca	gira
	chair	break	cpm	child	fell

'The chair broke and the child fell'.

Ho

(33)	dubtea	rapuD	-ye	-n	-ete	hon	iyu$^{?}$	yen	-a	-e
	chair	break	pst	[-tr]	cpm	child	fell	-pst	-dec	-3sg

'The chair broke and the child fell'.

Let us analyse why (32) is ungrammatical in Hindi. The reason is simple. The INFL of the CP in Hindi is [-tensed] therefore it cannot assign case to the lexical subject (a lexical subject needs case).

Now let us see whey (33) is grammatical. The reason again is simple. The INFL of the CP in Ho is [+tensed], hence it has the capacity to assign case to the lexical subject. Once the lexical subject of the CP clause gets case the construction becomes perfectly grammatical.

Hindi-Urdu (Indo-Aryan)

(34)	*baariS	ho-	kar	ole	gir	rahe	hɛ
	rain	occur	cpm	hailstones	falling	are	

'It rained and hailstones are falling'.

Ho

(35)	gamaa	ke	-D	-ete	aaril	iyu$^{?}$	-tan – a
	rain	pst	[+tr]	cpm	hailstones	fell	prog decl

'It rained and the hailstones are falling'.

The explanation which is given for (32) and (33) is valid for (34) and (35) also. In such constructions the IDENTITY CONSTRAINT is violated.

The position of PRO in a conjunctive participial construction in Ho

(36)	biru$_i$	[PRO$_i$	nokri	bagi-	ke-	(D-)	ete]	esupure	hiatiŋ	-yen	-a
	Viru		job	leave	pst	([+tr])	cpm	very	sad	-pst	dec

'Biru became very sad after leaving the job'.

In (36) PRO is the subject of the CP clause which occurs to the right of the subject of the matrix clause which is biru 'Viru'.

(37)	[PRO$_i$	nokri	bagi	-ke	-D	-ete]	biru$_i$	esupure	hiatiŋ	-yen	-a
		job	leave	pst	[+tr]	cpm	Viru	very	sad	-pst	-dec

'Viru became very sad after leaving the job'.

In (37) PRO is to the left of the matrix clause.

In So:ra: an infinite form of the verb which corresponds to the indeclinable past perfect participle is used as a conjunctive participle. It is formed by means of the suffix *–le* as following:

(38) jum	-le
eat	-cpm

'having eaten'

23. Reduplication and Compound

(39a) owa$^{?}$ owa$^{?}$ re
house house in
'in every house '

(39b) anjaa -anjaa
quick quick
'quickly'

(40a) kom te kom
little than little
'at least '

(40b) bugin bugin kiteb -ko
good good book IIIpl
' very good books'

Sentence (39) shows that the reduplication of noun forms plural form.

In the case of reciprocals usually both parts of the verb are given the *–pV-* infix (Deeney 1966).

(41a) ti-pi: ipid 'take each other by the hand'
(41b) ha-pa-l –u-pu-ra 'repay each other.'
(41c).ka-pa-ji –ha-pa-l 'take back to one another'

In all cases of reflexives only the second part of the compound verb is given the reflexive ending *–n.*

(42a) tingu –ura-n
stand –again-VR
'stand again

(42b) tai –antaa-n
remain –in the mean while-VR
'remain in the mean while'

(43c) lo -goe$^{?}$ -n
burn –kill-Vr
'burn onself to death'

Actions habitually done could be expressed by reduplicating the first consonant and bowel, or lengthening the first vowel. In the case of compound verbs this is done only to the second part of the compound verb as the followings (Deeney 1966):

(44a) jōjom 'repeatedly eat'
(44b)sesen ' repeatedly walk'
(44c) ēm 'habitually give'
(44d) dēnga 'habituallu help'

(45a) sab -tāb

catch –quicky

'habitually catch hold of quickly'

(45b) em -ūra

give -back

'habitually give back'

In the first class of compond verbs, the modifying roots generally bear the same meaning as when they are used separately. This method of forming compounds by the junction of two separate roots is very common in Ho.

The modifying roots may sometimes have meanings different fom those attaching to them when standing by themselves, and in a few cases, they have even ceased to be used independently.

(46) pro hola -e paiti -ete -keD-a

he yesterday -3sg work –start -pst –dec

'He started work yesterday.'

(47) pro [jom -chaba -ke -te] -e ol -ean -a

he eat -finish -pst -cpm –3sg go out –pst -dec

'He finished eating and went out.'

(48) hatu -te idi -agu -i -me

village-to take –bring –3sg-imperative

'Take him to the village and bring him back.'

(49) am huju -ura -re owa$^?$ -te -ñ rua -^{w}a

you come-back –when house –to –1sg return-dec

'When you come back, I will return home.'

As we can see, the object agreement marker always occurs to the right of the second word. And the transitive verb, the adverb and postposition can be compounded with the the verb in Ho.

In Mundari there are three ways of compounding to form a stem: a) compounding of two transitive roots, b) compounding of a root and postposition, and c) compounding of the secondary internally changed forms.

(50a) kaji -deŋga
say -help
'to plead'

(50b) jom –la?
eat -in excess
'eat in excess'

(50c) bara -bari
equal -euqal
'to equal'

Repetition of a word or a part of it is a common linguistic process in So:ra:. The roots of some verbs are necessarily re-duplicated when they are conjugated as the followings:

(51a) di –di 'to count'
(51b) mel-mel 'to inspect'

In Santhali when the whole verbal stem is reduplicated, it can be combined with any of the auxiliary suffixes. They are added to the second element. The total reduplication signals intensified or continued action, or it indicates that the action nearly happened, but did not finally.

Santhali (Tibeto-Burman)
(52a) lukut -lukud -ok -kan -a
tremble-tremble –MID-IPFV-IND
'was trembling'

(52b) landa-landa-y-et -a
laugh-laugh-y-IPFV-IND
'laughed'

Compound stems consist of a root and one or more other elements(verb roots or adverbs) in Santhali.

(53a) dal -goc
beat-kill
'beat to death'

(54b) dis-am
remember-find
'remember and find'

In Santhali there is also manner compound: the second root specifies the manner of the action described by the first root.

(55a) sap-uric
hold-tightly
'hold tightly'

(55b) gu-bi
bring-enough
'bring enough'

24. Causative construction

By causative verbs mean causing or making or having someone do something. Likewise, the causative markers *iri* or *ici* may be added to the transitive roots as well as the intransitive roots, and are permissive in character. In Ho there seems to be no morphological pattern for causative constructions. Thus after the causative marker is incorporated into the verb we find the 'transitivizing effect'.

(1)	pro_i	uli	$-i\tilde{\tilde{n}}_i$	jom	-keD	-a
	I	*mango*	*I sg*	*eat*	*pst*	*dec*

'I ate a mango. '

(2)	pro_i	hon	$-ko_j$	uli	$-i\tilde{\tilde{n}}_i$	jom	-iri	-keD	$-ko_j$	$-^{w}a$
	I	*child*	*pl*	*mango*	*I sg*	*eat*	*Cau*	*pst*	*Ⅲpl*	*dec*

'I fed a mango to children. '

(3)	pro_i	$sohan_x$	$-ta^{?}a$	-ete	hon	$-ko_j$	uli	$-i\tilde{n}_i$	jom	-iri	-keD	$-ko_j$	$-^{w}a$
	I	*Sohan*	*near*	*by*	*child*	*pl*	*mango*	*I sg*	*eat*	*Cau*	*pst*	*Ⅲpl*	*dec*

'I fed a mango to children by Sohan / I caused Sohan to feed a mango to children. '

This language contains two mechanism of causative construction i.e. morphological (by adding suffix *ici/ iri/dum* with the root of the verb) and lexical construction. The process of causative formation in Ho is very close to its sister language Santhali where the suffix $oco^{?}$ is added. The preceding discussion will make it clear that causativisation mainly by suffixical and in limited number of cases, by lexical causative.

(4)	$ini^{?}$	hon	nide	$-^{?}e$	giti	**ici**	ke	-D	-i	$-^{y}a$
	he	*child*	*night*	*3sg*	*sleep*	***caus***	*past*	*tr.*	*3sg*	*dec*

'He made child sleep at night'

(5)	am	ako	nide	-m	giti	**iri**	ke	-D	-ko	$-^{w}a$
	you	*they*	*night*	*2sg*	*sleep*	***caus***	*past*	*tr.*	*3pl*	*dec*

'you made them sleep at night'

(6) am sepeD uli -m jom **iri** ke -D-i -a

you boy mango 2sg eat ***caus*** *past tr-3sg dec*

'you made boy eat mango'

Lexical causative

Lexical causatives constitute a very limited set in this language.

Set A	Gloss	Set B	Gloss
nel	'to see'	*udub*	'to show'
paRaaw	'to read'	*eto*	'to teach'
hanDi	'to fall'	*sandang*	'to drop'
seno	'to go'	*kule*	'to send'
jom	'to eat'	*ajom*	'to feed'

Set A is related to set B such that set B is the causative Counterpart of Set A. According to McCawley and Lakoff, there are synonymy relations, lexical relations and entailment relations between them. hence *sandang* 'to show' Literally mean 'to make see' where as *nel* means 'to see by self'. Similarly *eto* means 'to make read' where as *paRaaw* means 'to read by self'. Thus the lexical causatives of set B are resulted to set A, in that they are causal verbs whereas verbs in A are non-causal.

A sentence containing a causative contains an extra NP argument then its corresponding non- causative counterpart i.e. number of syntactic argument increases as shown in the pair of sentences below.

(7a) hon sutui-e nel tan -a

child shirt-3sg see pres. dec

'Child is seeing the shirt.'

(7b)	dada	hon	sutui	-e	udub	tan -e	-^{w}a
	father	*child*	*shirt*	*3sg*	*show*	*pres-3sg*	*dec*

'Father is showing shirt to child.'

(8a).	puti	tebul	-re-te	iyu$^{?}$	ke	-n	-a
	book	*table*	*from*	*fall*	*pst.*	*- in tra.*	*dec*

'The book fell from the table.'

(8b).	añ	puti	tebu	-re-ñ	iyu$^{?}$	ke	-D	-a
	I	*book*	*table*	*on-1sg*	*drop*	*past*	*tr.*	*dec*

'I dropped book on the table.'

(9a).	ako	owa$^{?}$	seno	tan	-a	-ko
	they	*home*	*so*	*pres. prog*	*decl.*	*3pl*

'They are going home.'

(9b).	ako	sepeD	owa$^{?}$-ko	kule	tan-e	-a
	they	*boy*	*home-3pl*	*send*	*pres-3sg*	*decl*

'They are sending boy to home.'

(10a).	borjuo	puti-e	paRaaw	ke	-D	-a
	Borjuo	*book-3sg*	*read*	*past*	*tr*	*dec*

'Borjuo read the book.'

(10b).	borjuo	hon-ko	puti-e	eto	ke	-D-ko	-^{w}a
	Borjuo	*child-pl*	*book-3sg*	*teach*	*past*	*tr-epl*	*dec*

'Borjuo taught the book to the children.'

Sentence (7a) the verb *nel* 'to see' has two arguments: the subject- *hon* 'child' and the object *Sutui* 'shirt' where as (7b) has an extra argument *dada*. Syntactically. there is a change in (7b) such that hon which is the subject of *nel* 'see' becomes the indirect object of *udub* 'to show' where as in the both *Sutui* 'shirt' is the direct object.

This implies a change in thematic relations in the both sentences: in (7a) *hon* 'child' is the agent but in (7b) *dada* 'father' is the agent where *hon* 'child' becomes or the "affected agent" or "subordinate agent"

Sentence (8a) is slightly different from Sentence (7a), as sentence (7a) contains a transitive verb i.e. verb i.e. two arguments a subject and a direct object but (8a) contains an in transitive verb with a single argument, that is the subject.

In sentence (5b), the causative verb 'sandang' has two arguments: a subject and a direct object, hence an extra NP as compared to its non-causative counterparts. Notice that in the set of intransitive sentences (8a) and its counterparts (8b) respectively. There is no change in thematic relation between the verb and its original subject. In both (8a) and (8b) *puti* 'book' remains the theme.

Comrie (1976) considered a causative sentence as having an underlying structure comprising of a matrix sentence having a subject NP corresponding to the "causer" e.g. *dada*-'father' in (7b) and an embedded sentence having a subject NP corresponding to the "causee" e.g. *hon* 'childern' in (7b). He also stated there is an accessibility hierarchy governing the grammatical relation which the embedded subject takes in the surface structure of a sentence.

Accessibility Hierarchy: Sub > DO.IO > OO

In this respect, we can see how the subject *hanDi-* 'fall' that is *puti* 'book' becomes the direct object of its causative counterpart **añ** 'I" in the absence of any other direct object. Similarly the subject of nel 'see', i.e. *hon* 'child' becomes indirect object of its causative counterpart *udub* 'to show' since *udub* 'to show' already has a direct object *sutui* 'shirt'.

Morphological Causative construction

In this language the major process of causativisation is morphological. It has a regular productive causative morphema **"ici"** which is attached to the root form of the verb to get a morphologically causativised verb. The morpheme is phonologically unconditioned. A list of verb which can be causativised through this regular productive morpheme is given below:

Noun -Causative	Gloss	Causative	Gloss
giti	'to sleep'	*giti-ici*	'to make sleep'
landa	'to laugh'	*landa-ici*	'to make laugh'
paiTi	'to work'	*paiTi ici*	'to make someone'
paRaaw	'to read'	*paRaaw ici*	'to make someone 'read
kule	'to send'	*kule-ici*	'to make someone 'send
ola$^{?}$a	'to write'	*ola$^{?}$aici*	'to make some one write'

Let us see some morphological causative construction

(11)	ini$^{?}$	hon	nide	-i	giti	ici	ke	-D-i	-^{y}a
	he	*child*	*night*	*3sg*	*sleep*	*caus*	*past*	*tr.-3sg*	*dec*

'He made child sleep at night.'

(12)	am	ako	hola-m	landa	ici	ke	-D-ko	-^{w}a
	you	*they*	*yesterday-2*	*laught*	*caus*	*past*	*tr.-3pl*	*dec*

'You made them laugh yesterday.'

(13)	sepeD	-ko	añ	esu	raa$^{?}$	ici	tan-iñ	-a
	boy	*pl.*	*I*	*very*	*weep*	*caus*	*pres prog-1sg*	*dec*

'Boys are causing me weep too much.'

(14)	añ	am	du^{w}er-ñ	nii$^{?}$	ici	ke	-D-me	-^{y}a
	I	*you*	*door-1sg*	*open*	*caus*	*past*	*tr.-2sg*	*dec*

'I made you open the door.'

The sentences (11) to (14) are caustivised sentences where the verb originally intranstitive is causativised by the morpheme '*ici*'. But in other sentences, it is somewhat different where we have another element i.e. instrumental '*taa ete'* 'through' (about it I have discussed in later section.) This might be due to the use of non-animate subject.

Double causatives

Double causatives are those causatives which need two extra NPs besides the agent or doer. Hence if as comrie say a causative verb needs one extra argument as compared to its non- causative counterpart, a double causative would need one extra argument as compared to its (single or first degree) causative. A double causative is employed to refer to indirect causation where the agent or doer not physically cause the event, but manipulate it through an intermediate agent, also on "instrumental agent"; hence in a double causative we have 'X made Y performs through Z'.

Ho shows double causative construction with the use of the regular causative morpheme ***ici/iri/dum***.

Verb	Gloss	Ist causative	Gloss	2nd causative	Gloss
rapuDi	'to break' intr	*rapuDi*	'to break tr.'	*rapuD ici*	'to make break?
boRako	'to boil' intr.	*boRako*	'to boil' tr.	*baRako ici*	'to make someone boil
ute	'to stand' intr.	*uTe*	'to make stand' tr.	*uTe ici*	'to make stand through someone
nii$^{?}$	'to open' intr.	*nii*	'to open' tr.	*nii ici*	'to make open'
hanDeD	'to close '	*hanDeD*	'to close' tr.'	*hanDeD ici*	'to make clear

Now let us consider the sentences below:-

(15a) da$^{?}$a boRakao tan -a
water boil pres.prog dec
'Water is boiling.'

(15b). ini-$^{?}$ da$^{?}$a -e boRakao ke- -D -a
she water 3sg boil pst tr. dec
'She boiled the water.'

(15c)	jon	ini?	ta?a-ete	da?a	boRakao	ici	ke	-D	-a
	jon	*she*	*through*	*water*	*boil*	*caus*	*pst*	*tr*	*dec*

'Jon made her boil the water.'

(16a).	dubtea	rapuD	eyn	-a
	chair	*break*	*pst*	*dec*

'The chair broke.'

(16b)	am	dubtea	-m	rapuD	ke-	-D
	you	*chair*	*2sg*	*break*	*past*	*tra.*

'You broke the chair.'

(16c)	añ	am	dubtea-ñ	rapaD	ici	ke-	-D-em	-a
	I	*you*	*chair-1sg*	*break*	*caus*	*past*	*tra-2sg*	*dec*

I made you break the chair.'

In these sentences we have a set of morphological causatives where the non-causatives verb (or intrasitive form) is not different from the causative (or transitive form).

Verb	Gloss	Causative	Gloss
giti	'to sleep'	*giti ici*	'to make someone sleep
paRaaw	'to read'	*parRaaw ici*	'to make someone read
ema	'to give'	*ema ici*	'to make someone given
kule	'to send'	*kule ici*	'to make someone send
paiTi	'to do'	*paiTi ici*	'to make someone do'

The verb which is a double causative is hence eaisly formed with the regular morphological causative suffixed to the causativised form. In order to form double causative form verb we simply and ici to the tranitivised verb- verb + regular causative morpheme = verb with double causation.

Not that in construction above mentioned containing a double causative, the instrumental form in tea etc 'through/by' is added to clarify the meaning. It is not permitted to drop this form in this language unlike Ladakhi in which instrumental from '*Zeste*' 'through is generally avoided. But if one will drop it in another language like Ladakhi language the meaning will be different but in this language we do not get any difference.

(17a)	jon	ini-$^{?}$	ta$^{?}$a-ete	da$^{?}$a	boRakao	ici	ke	-D	-a
	John	*he*	*through*	*water*	*boil*	*caus*	*pst*	*tra*	*dec*

'John caused water boil through him.'

(17b)	jon	ini$^{?}$	da$^{?}$a	boRakao	ici	ke	-D-i	-^{y}a
	John	*he*	*water*	*boil*	*caus*	*pst*	*tr-3sg*	*dec*

'John made him boil water .'

(18a)	añ	am	ta$^{?}$a-ete	dubtea-ñ	rapuD	ici	ke	-D	-a
	I	*you*	*through*	*chair-1sg*	*break*	*caus*	*pst*	*tr*	dec

'I mad you break the chair'

(18b)	añ	am	dubtea	rapuD	iri	ke	-D-me	-a
	I	*you*	*chair*	*break*	*caus*	*pst*	*tr-2sg*	*dec*

'I made you break the chair.'

Here we are not getting any difference in the meaning of (17a) and (17b) and the same is the case with (18a) and (18b). Here (17b) and (18b) instrumental marker has been dropped but still the meaning what we are getting is same what we are getting from (17a) and (18a). In this language it is permissible. But there are certain languages in the world where this phenomenon is not permissible.

Here one more very important thing is happening in these sentences due to the characteristics of verb. In earlier we have seen that when we use instrumental form ***ta$^{?}$a ete*** generally we have there animate subject which have the role of agent in sentence.

A Note on Animate and Non-animate subjects regarding Causative formation.

In order to express causativized expression we have to be careful regarding the characteristics of verb whether it is transitive or intransitive and whether the subject of intransitive verb is animate or non-animate which affects the use of causative marker ici/ini/ dum in sentence. Let us see some sentences:-

(19a)	añ	nide	-ñ	giti	-yen	-a
	I	*night*	*1sg*	*sleep*	*pst*	*dec*

'I slept at night.'

(19b).	hon	añ	nide	-i	giti	ici	ke	-D-iñ	-^{y}a
	child	*I*	*night*	*3sg*	*sleep*	*caus*	*pst*	*tr.-1sg*	*dec*

'Child made me sleep at night'

(19c)	ako	hon	ta$^{?}$a -ete	añ	nide	ko	giti	ici	ke-D-iñ	-a
	they	*child*	*through*	*I*	*night*	*3pl*	*sleep*	*caus*	*pst-1sg*	*dec*

'They made me sleep through child.'

(20a).	due^{w}r	nii$^{?}$	tan	-a
	door	*open*	*pres*	*dec*

'The door opens.'

(20b).	abu	due^{w}r-bu	nii$^{?}$	tan	-a
	we	*door-1pl*	*open*	*pres*	*dec*

'We open the door.'

(20c)	teresa	abu	ta$^{?}$a –ete	due^{w}r-e	nii$^{?}$	ici	tan	-a
	Teresa	*we*	*through*	*door-3sg*	*open*	*caus*	*pres.*	*dec*

'Teresa causes us open the door.'

Verb in incorporation

According to Baker, in corporation is a process by which an argument is incorporated in another. He also states that one semantically independent word comes to be inside another. The formation of the larger unit will take place at the syntactic level because movement, which is a syntactic process will bring the two units together. As a consequence, in corporation

1. Creates a complex category at the zero level or lexical level.
2. It creates a syntactic link between two positions in the phase marker.

In the process, verb incorporation brings change in grammatical functions of NPs. Let us now see the structural possibilities for morphological causatives in HO through the process of Verb incorporation.

Ho causative construction can be divided into lexical and morphological. The lexical causatives in Ho constitute a limited set. From the non-causative to the causative sentence there is a charge in the thematic relations where subject/agent of non-causative sentence becomes the object of non-causative sentence becomes the object/patient in the lexical causative counterpart. As far as, the morphological causatives are concerned, they can be regular and double causatives.

Regular causatives verbs are produced by adding the causative suffix ***ici/ini/ dum*** to the verb to causativise it. Double causative in the case of single causation verbs, they are formed by use of ***ta*ˀ*a ete/ete*** (instrumental) as well s the causative form. In other cases e.g. lexical double causatives are formed by suffixing ***ici/ini/dum*** to the lexical cuasatives.

25. Case marker

In Ho there is no direct object case marker (Accusative) and no indirect object case marker (Dative)[31].

(21) pro$_i$ pro$_j$ mi^{y}ed uli– iñ $_i$ em– a– m $_j$ –tan –a

I you one mango Isg give epen IIsg prog dec

'I am giving one mango to you. '

(22) pro $_i$ añ- ta$^?$a kui-hon- ko $_j$ kul– keD– ko $_j$ -^{w}a -ben $_i$

you.polite me near girl pl send pst IIIpl dec IIdual

'You sent girls to me. '

In (22) *–ta$^?$a* is not a dative marker. It is a kind of adverbial postposition which functions as a suffix. Consider the following examples:

(23) pro$_i$ pro$_j$ mi^{y}ed' uli -iñ $_i$ em -aD -mi $_j$ -^{y}a

I you one mango I sg give pst.pef IIsg dec

'I had given a mango to you. '

(24) añ en -ta$^?$a (-re) tai -^{y}o -^{w}a

I that near in be emph dec

'I will be there '

(25) nen -ta$^?$a isu rabaŋ- (min)- a

this near very cold is dec

'It is very cold here '

In Ho we can find Exceptional Case marking as the following example:

(26) pro$_i$ añ-te-ge murku -ge -ñ̃ $_i$ addan -tan -a

I myself smart emph I sg believe is dec

'I belive myself to be smart. '

---

[31] But some of Ho people, mostly young people use *–ke* as an Acc and a dative marker.

According to Neukom (1998), Santali nominals are marked for seven cases as the following table:

Case	Markers	e.g. with *kora* 'boy'	Functions
Nominative	*Ø*	*kora*	Subject. Object
Dative	*-then/-thec*	*kora-then*	IO, goal, possessor
Accusative	*-sen/-sec*		Destination, beneficiary
Instrumental	*-te*	*kora-te*	Instrument, cause
Ablative	*-khon/-khoc*	*kora-khon*	Source, seperation
Locative	*-re*	*kora-re*	Location
Genitive	*-ren/-reak, -rea*	*kora-ren/-reak*	possessor

Nouns and pronouns have no cases in So:ra:. The expressions that correspond to cases may be called case-phrases. The nominative form is frequently used as the accusative and dative in So:ra:.

26. Imperatives

Imperatives are formed by suffixing *–m*, *-ben* or *–pe* to the end of the sentence and the declarative marker *–a* must be deleted in the imperatives.

(27)	pro $_I$	gel	kui-hon	em	-añ $_i$	-me
	Me	*ten*	*girls*	*give*	*I sg*	*Imp*

'Give me ten girls !'

(28)	am $_I$	pro $_J$	sutui	alo	-m $_i$	em	-ko $_j$
	You	*them*	*shirt*	*never*	*IIsg*	*give*	*IIIpl*

'Do not give your shirt to them !'

In Santhali, imperative forms are distinguished from all other verb forms by two characteristic: they have no indicative marker –a, and the subject pronominal clitics are always attached to the verb form itself.

(29) am -do	oka -te	co-m	cala	-k	-kan	cala	-k	-me
you –TOP	where-ALL	ever-2sg	go	-MID-IPFV		go	-MID	–imper

'Please, do go wherever you go.'

27. Participle

The head noun must govern the participle form from right to left in Ho. Forming a participle in Ho is that a declarative marker *–a* must be dropped and then the intransitive marker *–n* occurs with the past tense marker instead of the transitive marker *–D* in the perfect participle. And in the imperfect participle the progressive marker *–tan* occurs to the verb. Hence there is no specific particle form in Ho.

(30)	pro$_i$	ra$^?$	-tan	hon$_j$	ge	-ñ̃$_i$	tam	-ki	-e$_j$	-^{y}a
	I	*cry*	*prog*	*child*	*emph*	*I sg*	*hit*	*pst*	*IIIsg*	*dec*

'I hit the crying boy. '

(31)	seno	-^{y}en	din	ka	uju	-e
	go	*pst*	*day*	*not*	*return*	*dec*

'Gone day never returns. '

(32)	cigaareT	sip	-do	homo	laged'	isu	karab	-a
	cigarette	*smoke*	*emph*	*health*	*for*	*very*	*bad*	*dec*

'Smoking is injurious to health. '

In (30) only verb is used for participle. In Ho bare root form without any affixation is an infinitive, which when placed before a noun performs the function of an adjective. Some transitive and intransitive verb roots are formally identical.

(33a)	añ	-a	seno
	I	*gen*	*go*

' my going '

(33b)	am	-a	jom
	you	*gen*	*eat*

' your eating '

(33c)	ako	-^{w}a	susun
	they	*gen*	*dance*

' their dancing '

(34)	huju$^?$ -tan	ho	apu-ñ
	come –prog	*man*	*father-1sg*

'The man who is coming is my father.'

(35)	nir	-eyan	ho -kiŋ	keya	-ura -kiŋ -me
	run	*-pst*	*man –dual*	*call*	*-back –dual-IMP*

'Call back the two men who ran away.'

(36a) am goe? –keD kula -kiŋ aguʷa –ñ -me

you kill -pst tiger –dual bring -1sg –IMP

'Bring me the two tigers which you killed.'

* (36b) am goe? -keD-kiŋ kula –kiŋ aguʷa –ñ -me

you kill -pst -dual tiger –dual bring -1sg –IMP

'Bring me the two tigers which you killed.'

28. Verb *Be* and Tense

In this section we shall analyze various functions of verb "be" in HO in order to generalize some issues through various instance with examples. However it is unclear to distinguish the usage of *–min* and *–tan* in verb 'be' in Ho. And we will see some other functions of verb 'be' *-tan* as a tense marker and an aspect marker.

Thus if we see the past form of the verb 'be' is *–taiken* 'was'. Here *–taiken* can be broken into *tai* 'to stay' and *ken* 'simple past tense'. Moreover the past continuous form is *–tan taiken* ' was ~ing'. Hence we may think that *–tan* is a sort of aspect marker rather than a verb 'be' in Ho.

Identification

(37)	jon	añ	-a	guru	min[32]	-a
	John	*I*	*gen*	*teacher*	*Is*	*dec*

'John is my teacher.'

(38)	Jon	añ-a	guru	tan	-a
	John	*my*	*teacher*	*is or aspect.mkr*	*dec*

'John is my teacher.'

(39)	jon	añ-a	guru	Ø
	John	*my*	*teacher*	

'John is my teacher.'

The examples above show that verb 'be' in Ho can be dropped in the present tense as in Bengali and most of Dravidian languages. However the absence of verb 'be' is not compulsory in Ho. But in unmarked sentence it is usually absent as in (39).

---

[32] Actually it is kind of controversial to argue that verb 'be' in Ho is ***min***. According to J.Deeney it is ***mina*** in Ho. But I shall argue that it is ***min***. Because the past form of verb 'be' does not show ***–a*** ,and another types of verb 'be' or aspect marker in Ho is also ***tan***. Even though we may explain that ***–a*** is deleted due to the collision of the declarative marker ***–a*** : ***mina*** + ***a*** ⇒ ***mina***

(40)	jon	añ	-a	juRi	tai kin	-a
	John	*I*	*gen*	*friend*	*was*	*dec*

'John was my friend.'

However sentence (40) indicates that verb 'be' cannot be dropped in the past tense.

Class Membership

(41)	raam $_i$	ukil	(min/tan	-a	-i $_i$)
	Ram	*lawyer*	*is*	*dec*	*3.sg*

'Ram is a lawyer.'

Verb 'be' in Ho is sort of dropped in the present tense. But if it is not dropped the subject agreement marker occurs to the right of the declarative marker as in (41).

Class Inclusion

Here we see Class inclusion in terms of [±animate]

(42)	sita	kuihon	(min/tan	-a	-i $_i$)
	Sita	*girl*	*is*	*dec*	*3.sg*

Sita is a girl.

(43)	puti	ka	- ø	kui-hon
	book	*not*		*girl*

'A book is not a girl'

Sentence (42) shows that verb 'be' in the form of *–min* and *–tan* both is also dropped in Class inclusion. Moreover in negative sentence, verb' be is also dropped as in (43).

Demonstrative

(44a) en juRi añ̃ -a bugin ø -a
that friend I gen good dec
'That friend is good.'

(44b) en juRi añ -a bugin -min -a
that friend I gen good is dec
'That friend is good'

Apart from the demonstrative cases sentence (44a) shows the absence of verb 'be' while in sentence (44b) verb 'be' occurs after an adjective. This is due to that verb 'be' can also be dropped in the present tense when the predicate is adjective. However instead, if we put *–tan* after the adjective that expression is not proper sentence in Ho. Thus *–min* must occur after the adjective as a verb 'be'.

Participle formation

Verb 'be' may be used in the formation of three types of participle constructions are found in general. Here we can also understand the functions of verb 'be' in participle constructions.

Adjective participle

In Ho declarative marker *–a* is obligatory dropped to make a participle structure. Instead verb 'be' must be exhibited in the participle structure. However only *tan* can be used in this case. Because tan also functions as a aspect marker in Ho as illustrated in:

(45) pro $_i$ jom -e -tan -a - ñ $_i$
I eat 3.sg prog dec 1.sg
'I am eating.'

* (46) pro ᵢ jom -e -min -a - ñ ᵢ

I eat 3.sg prog dec 1.sg

'I am eating.'

Thus when verb be is used as an aspect marker only tan can be occurred in Ho. So verb 'be' *-tan* in Ho also functions as tense marker as well as aspect marker in Ho. And another verb 'be' *-min* cannot be used for tense or aspect in HO as shown in (46).

(47)a. da$^?$a hari tan -a

water flow prog dec

'Water is flowing' - slope

(47)b. da$^?$a seteñ tan -a

water flow prog dec

' ater is flowing' - high

Sentences (47a) and (47b) indicate the distinction between the high and the slope. However verb 'be' *–tan* functions like 'be + ing' in English in the examples above. And the following examples may show that only verb 'be' can be used for participle structure in Ho. And the order of constituents is, of course, changed to modify the head noun.

(48)a. hari - tan da$^?$a(slope)

flow prog/verb 'be' water

'flowing water'

(48)b. jom -tan ho

eat prog man

'the man who is eating'

Adverbial Participle

Just as in Adjective Participles, the form of verb 'be' *-tan* itself but without the declarative marker *–a* is also used to form Adverbial participle.

(49) ini? jom -tan -ø rew jagar tan -taiken -a

she eat prog dec while talk prog was dec

'She was talking while eating.'

In sentence (49) we can see two different functions of verb be *-tan*. One is a verb 'be' + a progressive marker : is + ing ,and the other is as a participle without the occurrence of the declarative marker *–a.*

Predicative Perfect Participle:

Another participle construction in which verb 'be' plays a role is the predicative perfect participle. In these constructions again, the past form of verb 'be' is used for predicative perfect participle in Ho.

(50) pro $_i$ puti -ñ̃ paRaaw -tan tai ken -a

I book 1.sg read prog was dec

' I was reading a book '

Tense marker

In this section we will roughly discuss tense markers in Ho. As we have seen earlier, there is a transitive marker-*D* and intransitive marker *-n*. Here in the present tense verb 'be' *–tan* plays a role as a tense marker and an aspect marker.

Tense	Transitive Verb	Intransitive Verb
Future Tense	*Ø*	*Ø*
Present Tense	*-tan*	*-tan*
Progressive	*-tan*	*-tan*
Past Progressive	*-tan tai ken*	*-tan tai ken*
Simple Past	*-keD*	*-ken /yen*
Present Perfect	*-akaD*	*-akan*
Past Perfect	*-leD / -laD*	*-len*

Future

(51) pro $_i$ mi^{y}ad   puti-ñ$_i$ paRaaw   -a

I   one   book-1sg   read   dec

'I will read a book.'

Present

(52)pro $_i$ miyad   puti-ñ$_i$ paRaaw   tan   -a

I   one   book-1sg   read   pres   dec

'I read a book.'

Progressive

(53)pro $_i$ miyad   puti-ñ$_i$ paRaaw   tan   -a

I   one   book-1sg   read   prog   dec

'I read a book.'

Past Progressive

(54) pro $_i$ manDi   -m $_i$ jom   -tan   taiken   -a

you   food   2.sg   eat   prog   was   dec

'You were eating food.'

Simple Past

(55) pro $_i$ manDi   -m $_i$ jom   ke   -D   -a

You   food   2.sg   eat   pst   [+tr]   dec

'I ate food..'

(56) pro $_i$ añ-a   juRi $_j$–m$_i$ nel   -ke   D   -i $_j$ -^{y}a

you   my   friend-2sg   see   pst   [+tr]   3sg   dec

'You saw my friend.'

In the past tense we need to see the role of [±animate] of the object in Ho. While object agreement marker occurred to the right of the tense marker in (56) due to the [+animate] object, no object agreement marker occurred to the verb in (55) due to the [-animate] object.

Present Perfect

(57) pro $_i$	añ-a	juRi $_j$-m	nel	-aka	-D	-i $_j$	-^{y}a
you	*my*	*friend-2sg*	*see*	*pres.pef*	*[+tr]*	*3sg*	*dec*

'You have seen my friend.'

Past Perfect

(58) pro $_i$	añ-a	juRi $_j$-m	nel	-la	-D	-I $_j$	-^{y}a
you	*my*	*friend-2sg*	*see*	*pst.pef*	*[+tr]*	*3sg*	*dec*

'You had seen my friend.'

With the auxiliary verb 'can'

(59)añ $_i$	miyad	puti	ñ$_i$	paRaaw	dai	-^{y}a
I	*one*	*book*	*1.sg*	*read*	*can*	*dec*

'I can read a book.'

With the auxiliary verb 'have to'

(60)añ $_i$	mi^{y}ad	puti	-ñ̃ $_i$	paRaaw	tia	durkar	-a
I	*one*	*book*	*1.sg*	*read*	*to*	*have*	*dec*

'I have to read a book.'

Locative

Here, verb 'be' has also got the function of locative marker. It is used for location of time and space as illustrated in:

(61) en	tebul	re	ba	min	a
that	*table*	*on*	*flower*	*is*	*dec*

' The flower is on that table'

In Ho language there is no any expletive construction. Thus subject NP occurs either the initial position or preverbal position and verb 'be' functions as a locative marker.

Existential

In this construction the verb 'be' is used as a complement-les verb in only very special contexts, asserting the existence of some being of thing. The following philosophical sentences are examples of Ho language:

(62a) bagawan min / tan -a
god *exist s* *dec*
'God exists'

(62b) bagawan -ø
god *exists*
' God exists'

Though it is existential construction verb 'be is also dropped in the present tense in Ho as illustrated in (62b).

Physical state:

* (63)a. añ hasu tan -a
I *sick* *is* *dec*
'I am sick..'

(63)b. añ hasu min -a
I *Sick* *is* *dec*
'I am sick.'

Sentence (63b) is good evidence to support that min is used not with the adjective but with the noun.

In Ho there is no dative subject construction due to the absence of the dative case marker. But in some cases null-dative subject construction is appeared. However from the examples above we can illustrate that verb 'be' is also occurred for a physical or mental state in Ho.

Mental temperament

(64) ini	esu	kurkur	re	Ø
he	*very*	*upset*	*emph*	*verb.be*

'He is upset.'

In these cases verb 'be' does not occur. But the occurrence of verb 'be' is optional in Ho.

29.Thematic Relation

The θ-roles assigned to constituents within the VP are called internal θ-roles; these constituents are called internal arguments. The θ-role assigned to the subject is called the external ɵ-role, and the subject of a sentence is called the external argument. In addition, the set of argumentts, their properties, their relations to one another, and their role in the syntax is called argument structure. As already known in theta criterion that each argument bears one and only one θ-role, and each θ-role is assigned to one and only one argument (Chomsky 1981:36). To identify the thematic roles in Ho I will adapt the definition of the thematic role by Liliane Haegeman (1994:49-50):

A) Agent: The one who intentionally initiates the action expressed by the predicate.

(65)	raam	pro $_i$	tam	-iñ $_i$	-tan	-a
	ram	*me*	*hit*	*1sg*	*pres*	*dec*
	<Agent>					

'Ram hits me.'

(66)	pro $_i$	pro $_j$	cereb	ke	-D	-am $_j$	-a	-ñ $_i$
	I	*you*	*kiss*	*pst*	*[+tr]*	*2sg*	*dec*	*1sg*
	<Agent>							

'I kissed you.'

From the above examples we can see that the subject NPs *raam* 'Ram' in (64) and *pro$_i$* 'I' in (65) are assigned the θ-role of Agent by the verb *-tam* 'hit' and *–cereb* 'kiss', respectively.

B) Patient: The person or thing undergoing the action expressed by the predicate.

(67)	pro $_i$	pro $_j$	tam	-ke	-D	-mi $_i$	-^{y}a	-^{y}e
	he	*you*	*hit*	*pst*	*[+tr]*	*2sg*	*dec*	*3sg*
		<Patient>						

'He hit you.'

(68) ini$^?$ pro$_i$ cereb -ki -mi$_i$ -a

he you kiss pst 2sg dec

<Patient>

'He kissed you.'

(69) añ mi^{y}ad kadal$_i$ jom -e$_i$ -tan -a

I one banana eat 3sg prog dec

<Patient>

' I am eating a banana.'

From the above examples it is clear that the object NPs in (67), (68) and (69) are assigned the -role of patient. In (67) *pro$_j$* 'you' is assigned patient θ-role by the verb *tam* 'hit.' In (68) *pro$_j$* 'you' is also assigned patient θ-role but by the different verb in this it is assigned by the verb *cereb* 'kiss.' However in (69) *kadal* 'banana' is assigned the patient θ-role by the verb *jom* 'eat.'

C) Theme: The person or thing moved by the action expressed by the predicate.

(70) pro$_i$ mi^{y}ad puti -ñ$_i$ paRaaw ø -a

I one book 1sg read future dec

<Theme>

'I will read a book.'

(71) pro$_i$ pro$_j$ nel -ke -D -mi$_j$ -^{y}a -ñ$_i$

I you see pst [+tr] 2sg dec 1sg

<Theme>

'I saw you.'

In (70) and (71) the direct object NPs *mi^{y}ad puti* 'the book', *pro$_j$* 'you' and *owa$^?$* 'house' are assigned the θ-role of theme which θ-marked by their verbs.

D) Experiencer: The entity that experiences some (psychological) state express by the predicate.

(72)	añ	haasu	-min	-a
	I	*sick*	*is*	*dec*
	<Experiencer>			

'I am sick.'

However there seems to be a non-nominative subject construction in Ho. Thus in case of experiencer subject they also use locative subject construction.

E) Goal: The entity towards which the activity expressed by the predicate is directed.

(73)	añ	-a	baba	pro$_i$	poesa	-em	-aD	-iñ$_i$	-^{y}a
	i	*gen*	*father*	*me*	*money*	*give*	*pst.pef*	*1sg*	*dec*
				<Goal>					

'My father had given money to me.'

In HO there is no dative case marker. However we can understand that *pro* 'me' is a Goal in (9).

F) Source: The entity from which something is moved as a result of the activity expressed by predicate.

(74)	pro$_i$	paTna	-te	-ñ$_i$	huju	-tan	-a
	I	*patna*	*from*	*1sg*	*come*	*pres*	*dec*
		<Source>					

'I come from Patna.'

G) Location: The place in which the action or state expressed by the predicate is situated.

(75)	ini$^?$	parkom	-re	giti$^?$	-^{y}an	-a
	he	*bed*	*on*	*sleep*	*pst*	*dec*
		<Location>				

'He slept on the bed.'

H) Instrument: The means by which an action is performed or something comes about.

(76)	pro $_{i}$	nutum	pencil	-te	-ñ $_{i}$	o:l	-ke	-D	-a
	I	*name*	*pencil*	*with*	*1sg*	*write*	*pst*	*[+tr]*	*dec*
			<Instrument>						

'I wrote my name with the pencil.'

In sentence (76) the PP *peccil-te* 'with the pencil' is an instrument theta-role and the occurrence of the postposition *–te* 'with' is obligatory in Ho.

I) Accompaniment

(77)	raam $_{i}$	siita $_{j}$	-lo$^{?}$o	puti	paRaaw	-ke	-D	-a	-kiŋ $_{i+j}$
	ram	*sita*	*with*	*book*	*read*	*pst*	*+[tr]*	*dec*	*3dual*
		<Accompaniment>							

'Ram read the book with Sita.'

(78)	añ $_{i}$	añ	-a	juRi $_{j}$	-te	mundo	sabindin	seno	-tan	-a	-liŋ $_{i+j}$
	I	*I*	*gen*	*friend*	*with*	*school*	*everyday*	*go*	*pres*	*dec*	*1dual*
			<Accompaniment>								

'I go to school with my friend everyday.'

The PP *siita-lo$^{?}$o* 'with Sita' in (77) and *añ-a juRi-te* 'with my friend' in (78), both are assigned the θ-role of accompaniment. They are arguments accompanying another argument *raam* 'Ram' and *añ* 'I', respectively. In this case of accompaniment , we may find that subject cannot give its agreement alone because of the incorporation. In other word when subject is accompanied by someone which is followed by a postposition *-lo$^{?}$o* or *–te* 'with' then the theta-role of Accompaniment is incorporated with the subject in Ho. Thus sentences (77) and (78) indicate that Accompaniment also functions as like a subject in Ho.

Ho verbs and their θ-Grid

Ho verbs in relation with the nature of thematic-roles they might have their thematic-grid[33]. There are three types of verbs in Ho:

1) Intransitive verbs that take one essential argument.
2) Transitive verbs that need two essential arguments.
3) Ditransitive verbs that need three arguments.

The term of essential argument is used for argument which must be overtly mentioned if the sentence is to be well-formed.

Verbs with one essential argument

Intransitive verbs of Ho can be classified in sub-groups on the basis of the nature of essential arguments they take.

Verbs that need only Agent as an essential argument

There are intransitive verbs that take agent as an essential argument. For instance, we can put verb such as *seno* 'to walk' in one sub-group, the subject of which has the agentive thematic relation with the verb we may look at (80) to illustrate this point:

(79) *seno* 'to walk': <Agent>

Here the verb *seno* 'to walk' assigns the thematic role of Agent, hence it requires only one argument due to the intransitive verb[34].

(80a)	pro$_i$	seno	-tan	-a	-bu$_i$
	we	*go*	*prog*	*dec*	*1pl*

'We are going.'

---

[33]In Government and Binding Theory , the thematic-grid is part of the lexical entry of the predicate which state which thematic-roles the argument of the predicate will bear , e.g. the verb 'kill' in English:
kill: < Agent, Patient>

[34] However in some cases an intransitive verb can take instigator, agent, patient etc in causative construction. We will discuss in detail later.

(80b) abu$_i$ mundo -bu$_i$ seno -tan -a

we school 1pl go prog dec

'We are going to school.'

From the above examples the subject NP *abu* 'we' is the argument of the verb *seno* 'to go' and has θ-role of agent in (80b). The PP *iskul* 'to school' is the location which it is not essential part of the θ-grid of the verb *seno* 'to go.' However, it gives additional information about the place of going to. The PP *mundo* 'to school' is called an adjunct[35].

Verbs that need Experiencer as an essential argument

Another type of intransitive verb that take experiencer as an essential argument rather agent. In addition, this type of verb we may also called psychological verb which express emotion, attitude or situation of one's mind. Lets consider the psychological verbs of Ho in (81) and (82):

(81a) *renge* 'to feel hungry': <Experiencer>

(81b) ini$^?$$_i$ renge -tan -e$_i$

he hungry pres dec + 3sg

'He feels hungry.'

(82a) *rããsa* 'to be happy': <Experiencer>

(82b) pro$_i$ ka$^?$ -e$_i$ $_{\text{rããsaa}}$ -tan -a

she neg mrk 3sg happy is dec

'She is not happy.'

In sentences (81) and (82) *ini$^?$*[36] 'he' and 'she' are the experiencers. They are the essential arguments for the verbs *renge* 'to feel hungry' and *rããsa* 'to be happy.' But former one is theta-marked by verb renge and latter one is theta-marked by adjective '*rããsa.*' Because *renge* occurs with the tense marker *–tan* whereas *raasa* does with the verb 'be.'

---

35 The normal constituent order of Ho is Sub-Adjunct-IO-DO- Verb.

36 In Ho, the 3sg pronoun 'he or she' have the same form i.e. *ini* used in farther distance while *a^{y}e* in nearer distance.

Verbs that take Theme as an essential argument

Ho has a group of verb which requires theme as an essential argument as following:

(83a) *apir* 'to fly' [-tr]: <Theme>

(83b) o^{w}e apir -e -tan -a

bird fly epen prog dec

'The bird is flying.'

Here the subject *o^{w}e* 'the bird' is the essential argument for intransitive verb *apir* 'to fly' which bear the θ-role of Theme.

Verbs with two essential arguments

The argument structure of a simple transitive verb consists of two obligatory arguments one is Theme / Patient as internal argument and the other is Agent as external argument. A transitive verb requires at least two essential arguments in general for their θ-grid. They are classified in sub-groups on the basis of the nature of the θ-role they might have.

Verbs that take Agent and Theme as an essential argument

Some transitive verbs take agent and theme as an essential argument:

i) Inchoative Verbs

They express the change of state of an entity. Inchoatives may be intransitives or transitive. If they indicate merely the change of the state, they are intransitives as in 'The door opened' but if they indicate what brought about the change of state, they are transitive as in 'I opened the door.' Lets consider inchoative verb in Ho as the following examples:

(84a) *handed* 'to close' [-tr]] : <Theme>

handed 'to close' [+tr] : <Agent, Theme>

(84b) $du^{w}er$ Handed $-^{y}e-$ -n -a

door close pst [-tr] dec

<Theme>

'The door closed.'

(84c) pro_{i} $du^{w}er$ $-eñ_{i}$ handed -ke -D -a

I door 1sg close pst [+tr] dec

<Agent> <Theme>

'I closed the door.'

(85a) *boRkaa* 'to boil' [-tr] : <Theme>

boRkaa 'to boil' [+tr] : <Agent, Theme>

(85b) $da^{?}a$ boRkaa $-^{y}e$ -n -a

Water boil pst [-tr] dec

'The water got boiled.'

(85c) $añ_{i}$ $da^{?}a$-ñ boRkaa -ka -D -a

I water-1sg boil pst [+tr] dec

'I boiled the water.'

Apart from the thematic relationship, when an intransitive verb is incorporated with the inchoative it becomes a transitive verb.

ii) Verbs of achievement

They involve unique and define time instances. Some verbs of achievement in Ho take agent and theme as their essential arguments. We may look at the verb *adaanaa* 'to know' as an example in (86):

(86a) *adan* 'to know' : <Agent, Theme>

(86b) konda jaanaa $ka^{?}e$ aadaan -tan -a

konda anything neg 3sg know pres dec

'Konda does not know anything.'

In (86) the argument *konda* 'Konda' is the agent and the argument *jaanaa* 'anything' is the theme. The agent alone is not sufficient to make it grammatical.

iii) Verbs of Accomplishment

They imply the notion of unique and definite time period. The verb of accomplishment will have not only an agent but also theme which is not necessary for an activity verb. The verbs of accomplishment in Ho also need two essential arguments. For example, we may look at the verb *paRaaw* 'to read' as in (87).

(87a) *paRaaw* 'to read': <Agent, Theme>

(87b)	pro$_i$	puti	-ñ̃$_i$	paRaaw	-tan	-a
	I	*book*	*1sg*	*read*	*prog*	*dec*

'I am reading a book.'

Here the subject NP *añ* 'I' has the θ-role of agent and the object NP *puti* 'book' has the θ-role of theme. While if the theme is deleted then the sentence becomes ungrammatical sentence in English it is also possible in Ho. However the property of the verb *paRaaw* 'read' has <Agent, Theme> in both languages. In brief, inchoative verbs, some verbs of accomplishment and achievement take agent and theme as their essential arguments.

Verbs which take Agent and Accompaniment

Ho has a class of verbs that take the θ-roles of agent and accompaniment. The term 'accompaniment' indicates a mutual dependence of action between two arguments in the sentence. A verb of this category needs the θ-roles of agent and accompaniment, as in:

(88a) *seno* 'to go': <Agent, Accompaniment>

(88b)	pro$_i$	am$_j$	-lo$^?$o	seno	-^{w}a	-laŋ$_{i+j}$
	I	*you*	*with*	*go*	*dec*	*1dual*

'I will go with you.'

In case of accompaniment it is not essential argument. In (88) the subject NP *pro$_i$(añ)* 'I' bears the θ-role of agent and the NP *am-lo$^?$o* 'with you' bears the θ-role of accompaniment. And we have already seen the phenomenon of accompaniment subject agreement marker is incorporated.

Verbs which take Experiencer and Theme as their essential arguments

Ho has verbs of physical and mental perception which require two essential arguments to have a well-formed sentence. We may look at the verb *raasaa* 'to like' and *nel* 'to see' as the following examples:

(89a) *rããsaa* 'to like': <Experiencer, Theme>

(89b)	pro$_i$	am	-a	undikui$_j$	-ñ$_i$	raasaa-	i$_j$-	tan-	a-
	I	*you*	*gen*	*sister*	*1sg*	*like*	*3sg*	*pres*	*dec*

'I like your sister.'

(90a) *nel* 'to see': <Experiencer, Theme>

(90b)	pro$_i$	hola	pro$_j$	nel	-a	-D	-mi$_j$	-^{y}a	-ñ$_i$
	i	*yesterday*	*you*	*see*	*pst.pef*	*[+tr]*	*2sg*	*dec*	*1sg*

'I had seen you yesterday.'

In (89) the subject NP *pro$_i$ (añ)* 'I' has the θ-role of experiencer and the object NP *ama uNdikui* 'your sister' has the θ-role of the theme as well as in (90) the subject NP *por$_i$(añ)* 'I' has the θ-role of experiencer and the object NP *pro$_j$(am)* 'you' has the θ-role theme. Both the object NPs in (90) and (91) are the essential arguments.

Verbs that need three arguments

A ditransitive verb requires three arguments .The θ-roles are given to two arguments within the VP are called internal θ-roles and the θ-role assigned to the subject is called the external θ-role which is external to VP. Ho has some ditransitive verbs that require three essential arguments in a sentence. The nature of these arguments depends on the lexical properties of the verb (i.e. its c-selection and s-selection properties).

Verbs which take Agent, Theme and Goal as essential arguments

The verb of this type describes the change of possession of an entity from one argument to another; they are verbs of transaction or exchange. They may take the agent and the theme in the form of an NP and the goal, either in the form of NP or a PP.

(91a)	*em*	'to give' :	<Agent, Theme, Goal>			
(91b)	pro $_i$	siita $_j$	puti	-ñ $_i$	em	-e	-^{y}a

(91a)	*em*	'to give' :	<Agent, Theme, Goal>				
(91b)	pro $_i$	siita $_j$	puti	-ñ $_i$	em	-e	-^{y}a
	I	*sita*	*book*	*1sg*	*give*	*3sg*	*dec*

'I will give a book to Sita.'

In (26a) the NP *añ* 'I' is the agent θ-role, the NP *kiteb* 'book' is the theme and the PP *siita* 'Sita' is the goal.

(92a)	*kul*	'to sent'	:	<Agent, Theme, Goal>				
(92b)	jon	marii $_j$	ciTTi	kul	le	D	-i $_j$	-^{y}a
	john	*mary*	*letter*	*send*	*pst*	*[+tr]*	*3sg*	*dec*

'John sent the letter to Mary.'

In (92) the NP *jon* 'John' is the agent, the NP *ciTTi* 'letter' is the theme and the PP *marii* 'Mary' is the goal.

Verbs with have Agent, Theme and Location as essential arguments

Ho has verbs of location that need agent, theme and location as essential arguments. With these verbs the agent and the theme are in the form of NPs and the location is in the form of PP. Let us consider the example below:

(93a)	*em*	'to put'	:	<Agent, Theme, Location>						
(93b)	pro $_i$	tebul	-re	-ñ $_i$	puti-ñ	em	-a	-ke	-D	-a
	I	*table*	*on*	*1sg*	*book-1sg*	*put*	*epen*	*pst*	*[+tr]*	*dec*

'I put a book on the table.'

In (93) the verb *em* 'put' takes three arguments: agent theme and location. In (94) the NP *pro* 'I' is the agent, the object NP *puti* 'book' is the theme and the PP *tebul-re* 'on the table' is the location.

However let us consider the following examples regarding to Case theory.

(94)	pro$_i$	am	-ta$^{?}$a	-re	hon	–ko$_j$ -ñ	em	-a	-D		-ko$_j$	-	^{w}a
	you	*near*	*to*	*child*	*3pl-1sg*		*give*	*pst.pef*	*[+tr]*		*3pl*		*dec*

' I had given children to you'

(95)	pro$_i$	pro$_j$	hon	–ko$_j$ -ñ	em	-a	-D	-mi$_j$	-^{w}a
	I	*you*	*child*	*3pl -1sg*	*give*	*pst.pef*	*[+tr]*	*2sg*	*dec*

'I had given you children.'

The above examples indicate that the dative case is structurally assigned in (94) but it is inherently assigned in (95). However both are theta-role of Goal.

Verbs that take Agent, Experiencer and Theme as essential arguments

This group of Ho verb takes agent, experiencer and theme as the essential arguments. It describes a verbal action that leaves a psychological impact on the experiencer. The impact is conveyed in the form of an IP but not a CP. We examine the verb *kaji* 'to tell' in (96) to illustrate the nature of θ-role it might have, as following:

(96a) *kaji* 'to tell' : <Agent, Experiencer,Theme>

(96b)	raam$_i$	jon	english	paRaaw	lagid-	-e$_i$	kaji-	ki-	^{y}a
	ram	*john*	*english*	*study*	*for*	*3sg*	*tell*	*pst*	*dec*

'Ram told John to study English.'

In (96) the verb *kaji* 'to tell' has the NP *raam* 'Ram' as subject and the NP *jon* 'John' and the IP PRO *english paRaaw-lagid* 'to study English'[37] as its complement. They bear the θ-roles of agent, experiencer and theme respectively. As the theme is in inside IP, its predicate *paRaaw* 'to study' has its own θ-grid such as Experiencer and Theme.

Thematic hierarchy in causative construction

In causative construction causative markers always occur to the right of the verb root.

(97)	raam$_i$	hon	-ko$_j$	(ta$^?$a)	-ete	a^{y}e	-a$^?$	paiti	-i$_i$	paiti	-ici -ko$_j$-^{w}a
	ram	*child*	*pl*	*near*	*by*	*his*	*gen*	*work*	*3sg*	*work*	*cau 3pl dec*

'Ram will cause children to do his work.'

In (97) there are three NPs. They are *raam* 'Ram' as an Instigator[38], *hon-ko* 'children' as an Agent, and *a^{y}e- a paiti* ' his work' as a Theme. But in examples below we find more complex thematic relationship due to the incorporation of the causative marker into the verb in Ho.

(98)	pro$_i$	a^{y}e$_j$	-ta$^?$a	-te	-ñ̃$_i$	pro$_x$	raa$^?$	-iri	-me$_x$	-tan	-a
	I	*him*	*near*	*by*	*1sg*	*you*	*cry*	*cau*	*2sg*	*pres*	*dec*

'I cause him to make you to cry. '

(99)	pro$_i$	a^{y}e$_j$	-ta$^?$a	-te	-ñ̃$_i$	pro$_x$	raa$^?$	-iri	-keD	-me$_x$	-a
	I	*him*	*near*	*By*	*1sg*	*you*	*cry*	*cau*	*pst*	*2 sg*	*dec*

'I caused him to make you cry.'

In (98) and (99) the causative construction in Ho needs only one verb with a causative to assign the theta roles to all NPs but in English it requires at least two

---

37 As we have seen earlier the root of the verb can be used as an infinitive form in Ho. Moreover it is followed by the postposition such as *laged'* or te or *ti^{y}a*.

38 Instigator Theta role: a person who causes something to happen.

verbs which can give the theta roles to all NPs in causative constructions. Thus we may reinterpret as the following:

Verb + *iri* : < Instigator, Agent, Goal/Recipient, Patient> in Ho

And in (100) *pro* 'I' can be an Instigator, *a^{y}e* 'he' is an Agent 1 and *pro* 'you' can be an Agent 2. However the following example shows the different thematic relationship.

(100)	raam	ako $_i$	ta$^?$a	te	mohan	ciTTi	ko $_i$	kule	-ici	-a	ko $_i$	-^{w}a
	Ram	*them*	*near*	*by*	*Mohan*	*letter*	*3pl*	*send*	*cau*	*tense*	*3pl*	*dec*

' Ram caused them to send a letter to Mohan'

Here, *raam* 'Ram' is an Instigator, *ako* 'them' is an Agent, *ciTTi* 'letter' is a Theme and *mohan* 'Mohan' is a Goal/Recipient. Thus in causative constructions we can say that only one verb can bear the thematic role of all NPs in Ho unlike in English. Moreover there seems to be a thematic hierarchy in terms of agreement. In (100) this sort of thematic relationship indicates that *ako* 'them' which is lexically case marked can bear its agreement inside verb while *mohan* 'Mohan' cannot though it is a Recipient since Agent is stronger than Goal/Recipient. And in (98) Agent is also stronger than Theme. But in (99) there are two Agents, here, we may think that Agent 2 is stronger than Agent 1 in terms of the occurrence of agreement. Because Agent 2 is theta marked by the main verb.

Hence the thematic hierarchy of Ho can be shown in below:

Agent > Goal/Recipient > Patient > Theme

Thus in this section, the analysis of the data has revealed that animacy plays an important role in relative clauses of the language, which we have seen from the formation of the relative pronouns; okoni (+ animate) and okona (- animate). Moreover, the relative clauses are externally headed and only postnominal. The possibilities of occurrence of RC are broadly used as in NP S2 VP and S2 NP VP but the construction of NP VP S2 is rarely used.

The study also has revealed that the full-fledged strategy can apply to all the NP positions on the accessibility hierarchy. In this strategy, the demonstrative adjective behaves like the definite article to indicate the definite head noun. In this language they do not use only the full-fledged strategy in modification but also the participial strategy which is prenominal and tensed.

There is an interesting point that I have found in the work is that a native speaker of Ho prefers using the participial strategy to the full-fledged one. Even though my analysis has shown that the relative-corelative construction is also found in Ho but the participial construction is preferable.

From my point of view, the correlative construction which is used in the language may be the result of language contact. Psychologically, a native speaker of Ho can use a participle phrase without hesitation, this means the strategy is very natural and easy to them to speak it out and it seems to be productive. On the other hand, they do not prefer the correlative construction which is also one of modification strategies. In my opinion, this should be a language contact situation. Since the area where we have collected data is a multilingual area, Hindi as the official language of the country which is used for education or political usage is of course more prestigious than the other languages. On the other hand, a language as Ho is spoken only in Ho.

30. Morphophonemic changes

Since Ho is an agglutinating language with words composed of one of more monosyllables, its segmentation into a syllable is easy. A morphemic boundary always coincides with the syllabic boundary, thus making a correlation between the morpho-phonemic and phonetic divisions. It is intended to give an account of the changes brought about in the affixes in Ho before giving for other types of affixes, specially the personal agreement markers, which exert a considerable influence on the forms of tense markers. A vowel constitutes the peak of a syllable and forms vocalic cluster within the same syllable in diphthong. No consonant cluster within a syllable. Here we may assume some patterns as illustrated in:

A) Elimination of the final consonant

Deletion of /d/ and in case of /e/ preceding /d/, deletion of /e/ is also possible. Since /d/ is preglottalized in all above cases, the glottal check remains even after insertion of /i/ as shown in tense + Ⅲsg marker.

a) *keD+ i* = *ki*$^{?}$ *i* or *ki*$^{?}$ or *ki*

b) *leD + i* = *li*$^{?}$ *i* or *li*$^{?}$ or *li*

c) *akaD +* *i =* *aki*$^{?}$*i* or *akai*$^{?}$ or *akai*

B) Introduction of glottal check

Apart from the transfer of checking by way of assimilation glottal check is freely introduced in Ho when the two vowels is coming together do not form a diphthong.

a) *ka + e* = *ka?e* or *kae ?* (negative + Ⅲsg)

b) *aye + a* = *aye?a* or *ayea?* (pronoun + possessive marker)

According to J.Deeney glottalization is phonemic in Ho. There are words where the meaning of the word is changed if a vowel is checked.

seta 'dog' *seta*$^{?}$ 'morning'

goe 'to wilt' *goe*$^{?}$ 'to kill

C) Vowel glides

a) /y/ insertion between i – a, i – e, a – e, e - a and i - o

mi + a = mi^{y}a

ki? + e = ki^{y}e

ge + a = ge^{y}a

Though there is a consonant between vowels glide can occur
iñ + a = iñ ^{y}a

b) /w/ insertion between o – a and u - a

ko + a = ko ^{w}a

huju + a = huju ^{w}a

D) Elision

Ho may lose either the preceding or the following vowel due to assimilation.

nel + laD = nel aD

em + laD = em aD

E) Vowel harmony

Roughly, harmony exists between two adjacent syllables.

a) if the preceding syllable has [a] the following frequently changes from [e] to [i].

b) if the following syllable has [i] but the preceding has [e] the later changes to [i]

F) Epenthesis

Roughly, /e/ occurs when only two consonants come together.

a) in case of postposition *–te/ -ete* : as a comparative marker and conjunctive participle marker etc.

b) if verb root ends a consonant *–e* occurs before tense marker. But in some cases *–e* is a direct object agreement marker.

a + i = e

(101) $(pro)_i$ iskul **-e** –te -ñ $_i$ huju ^{w}**a** ondo $(pro)_j$ jom **–e** -tan- **e** $_j$

I school epen from I sg come dec and he eat epen prog IIIsg+dec

'I am coming from the school and he is eating '

31. Declarative marker

According to L.Burrows, *–a* is a copular and J.Deeney says that it is a mood marker in Ho. But I shall argue that *–a* is a declarative marker. However we will discuss some evidence to support that argument in favor of the declarative marker.

A) In adverbial clause

(102) jaa-men-te pro $_i$ jaapa -m $_i$ seno –re -do, pro $_j$ kaji -^{y}eñ $_j$ -me

If you anywhere IIsg go con emph me say Isg imp

'If you go anywhere, say to me '

(103) owa$^{?}$ -ria bati -ñ jul -ke -D -re -ge cor nir -^{y}an -a

house of light Isg turn pst [+tr] con emph thief run pst dec

'As soon as I turned on the light the thief ran away.'

In (102) and (103) we find that there is no *–a* in each subordinate clause. So if we assume that *–a* is a declarative marker we can account for that since the declarative marker cannot occur in adverbial clauses.

B) In imperative sentence

(104) gel uri -ko em -a -ñ -ben

ten cow pl give epen Isg IIdual

'Give me ten cows '

(105) pro $_i$ alo -pe tam -iñ $_i$ -a

me do not IIpl hit Isg dec

'Do not hit me '

Both (104) and (105) are imperative sentences. But there is no declarative marker in (3) while there is that marker in (4) where prohibitions are expressed by the use of a special particle *alo* 'do not'. In (104) 2nd subject agreement marker cannot occur in preverbal position to avoid the confusion from declartive sentence. However in (105) 2nd subject agreement marker occurs to the preverbal word and the declarative marker also appears. We may account for that problem. Actually that sentence is a declarative sentence for prohibition expressed by the use of *alo*. Thus it functions as negative imperative sentence.

C) In conjunctive participle clauses

(106) pro $_i$ [PRO $_i$ huju -len -ete] [PRO $_i$ dub -ken -ete] jom -keD - a -ñ $_i$
I I come pst comp I sit pst comp eat pst dec Isg
'Having come and having sat, I ate '

The conjunctive participle *–ete/-te* occurs after the tense marker and declarative marekr *–a* is dropped in subordinate clause. And in conjunctive participle clause subject agreement marker cannot occur.

In addition, a declarative marker can occur in some cases of interrogative sentences. But in other cases it cannot occur. However, this element *–a* is not strictly bound with the stem, rather the aspect and tense markers are inserted between the two and in that case, it is suffixed to them.

32. Areal features

Ho language is spoken in Jharkhand and Orissa. In Jharkhand the official language is Hindi. Thus Ho people are bilingual. One of our informants who is from Jharkahnd is extremely influenced by Hindi. We may find a sort of interesting thing on the basis of his spoken Ho as in shown:

(107) ini $_j$ añ $_i$ -ke -ø $_j$ kiriŋ -kiD -in $_i$ -a

he me acc(?) buy pst I sg dec

'He bought me '

(108) añ biŋ -ke go$^?$e -ki$^?$ -e -ñ

I snake acc(?) kill pst dec I sg

'I killed a snake '

(109) añ $_i$ am $_j$ –ke añ -a -kuihon em -aD -me $_j$ -a -ñ $_i$

I you dat(?) my gen daughter give pst IIsg dec I sg

'I gave my daughter to you '

There is no accusative and dative case marker in Ho. However we find a kind of case marker from the examples above. That is *-ke* ' either dative or accusative case marker'. In Hindi *-ko* is a dative marker as well as accusative marker (or specificity marker). But instead of using *–ko* he changes the form to *–ke*. Because *–ko* is already existed in Ho as a plural marker. According to that informant it is common to use that kind of case marker in his town. And the following examples collected from the field work also show the influence of Hindi to Ho.

(110) añ $_i$ laD $_j$ -iñ $_i$ jom -e $_j$ -ti^{y}a -dorkar -a

I bread I sg eat IIIsg for must dec

'I must eat a bread '

(111) añ $_i$ laD $_j$ -iñ $_i$ jom -e $_j$ -ti^{y}a -min -a

I bread I sg eat IIIsg for 'be' dec

'I must eat a bread.'

(112) raam seno -ti^{y}a -min -a

Ram go for 'be' dec

'Ram has to go '

Though there is 'must' construction for the compulsory expression in Ho as shown in (110) they seem to copy Hindi structure by using the verb 'be' after the main verb in the same way as Hindi does.

33. The usage of the verb 'say'

It is significant to discuss the usage of the verb *mente* 'say' in Ho. This can be used as the followings:

A) in order to

(113) añ$_{i}$ Taj mahal nel mente agra -ñ$_{i}$ seno -^{y}an -a

I Tajmahal see to Agr I sg go pst dec

'I went to Agra to see Taj Mahal. '

B) Complementizer

(114) *pro* añ$_{i}$ ta$^{?}$a -re poesa bano -^{w}a] -^{w}e$_{i}$ mente kaji -^{y}an -ñ -a

he me near to money is not dec IIIsg comp say pst I sg dec

'He told me that he had no money.'

C) quotative

(115) haTo -re cikan -am kiriŋ e -^{y}a mente juRi -ñ kuli kiD -iñ -a

marketal in what you buy IIIsg dec Quot friend gen ask pst I sg dec

'My friend asked me " What will you buy in t he market?".'

34. The various usage of postposition *-te*

A) Possessive

The postposition *–te* acts as a genitive marker only for 3rd person, it occurs after the head noun possessive and pronominal possessive.

(116a)	bau–	te	(116b)	unDi–	te	(116c)	era–	te	
	elder brother	*his*		*younger brother*			*his*	*wife*	*his*
	'his elder brother'			'his younger brother'			'his wife'		

B) Comparison

It also functions as like a comparative adverb and subject agreement marker can be suffixed as shown in the following examples:

(117)	pro $_i$	baamai	-te	-ñ $_i$	jiliŋ-	a
	I	*Bamai*	*than*	*I sg*	*tall*	*dec*

'I am taller than Bamai. '

(118)	siita $_i$	somi	-te	-i $_I$	ceehra-	ge-	^{y}a
	Sita	*Somi*	*than*	*IIIsg*	*beautiful*	*emph*	*dec*

'Sita is more beautiful than Somi. '

(119)	kom	-te	kom
	small	*than*	*small*

'at least'

C) Conjunctive Participle Marker

The following example indicates that *–te* is also used as a conjunctive participle marker in Ho. In this case the verb occurs with only tense marker and the declarative marker cannot occur. Instead, conjunctive participle marker *–te* occurs as illustrated in:

(120) pro$_i$	[pro$_i$	huju	-len	-te]	[pro$_i$	Dub	-ken	-ete]	jom	-keD –a -ñ $_i$
I	*I*	*come*	*pst*	*cp*	*I*	*sit*	*pst*	*cp*	*eat*	*Pst dec I sg*

'Having come and having sat and I ate. '

D) Instrumental case marker and indicates the agency or means 'by' or 'with'.

-te 'by / with'

(121)

okon $_I$	cakuu $_i$	-te	pro$_j$	uutu	-ko $_j$	haaDe	-tan	-a	(en cakuu)	leser	-a
Which	*Knife*	*with*	*they*	*veg*	*IIIpl*	*Cut*	*prog*	*dec*	*that knife*	*sharp*	*dec*

'The knife with which they are cutting the vegetable is sharp. '

(122)	pro $_i$	jono	-te	seta	-ko	tam	-ki	-^{y}e
	they	*broom*	*by*	*dog*	*3pl*	*hit*	*pst*	*decl*

'They hit the dog by the broom.'

E) Comitative case marker

-te 'with'

(123)	aɕɜ $_i$	aɕɜ	-a	juRi $_j$	-te	iskul	sabindin	seno	-tan	-a	-liŋ $_{i+j}$
	I	*I*	*gen*	*friend*	*with*	*school*	*everyday*	*go*	*pres*	*dec*	*1dual*
				<Accompaniment>							

'I go to school with my friend everyday.'

In case of this example the postposition *–lo?o* can be substituted.

Ablative case marker

-te 'from'

(124)	aɕɜ $_i$	aɕɜ	-a	juRi $_j$	-te	iskul	sabindin	seno	-tan	-a	-liŋ $_{i+j}$
	I	*I*	*gen*	*friend*	*with*	*school*	*everyday*	*go*	*pres*	*dec*	*1dual*
				<Accompaniment>							

'I go to school with my friend everyday'.

(125)

okon$_i$	pro$_j$	bajar$_i$	(-re)	-te	uutu	-ko$_j$	kiriŋ	-keD	-a	sapa	-gi	-^{y}a
which	*they*	*market*	*in*	*from*	*veg*	*3pl*	*buy*	*pst*	*dec*	*clean*	*emph*	*dec*

'The market from which they bought the vegetable is clean. '

Locative case marker

-te 'in'

(126)a.

nen	-te
this	*in*

'in this'

(126)b.

en	-te
that	*in*

'in that'

in order to

(127)

raam$_i$	ondo	soma$_j$	nen	ta$^{?}$a -	ø	am	nel	-te	kin$_{i+j}$	huju	-len	-a
Ram	*and*	*soma*	*this*	*near*		*you*	*see*	*to*	*1sua*	*come*	*pst*	*dec*

' Ram and Soma came here to see you.'

In this sentence *–te* can be substituted by *laged'* 'for'

35. Passive

The internal argument of reflexives in Ho is a null argument or *pro*, which is an empty category. It may indicate that the verbal reflexive morpheme absorbs its internal argument. Thus, to a certain extent, the reflexive morpheme absorbs both the Case feature and the thematic relation in Ho. Reflexives and passives in Ho have something in common: both have the same morphological marker –n which is a detransitivizing marker occurring to the right of the verb.

However, it does not seem that they are homonymous. According to Burrows (1915), the passive is used very sparingly, the active form being the preferred choice. The morpheme -o[39] is a marker of the passives except in the past tense, where the active intransitive marker –n is used. The occurrence of the passive is permitted only with transitive verbs. Let us consider the following sentences.

(128a) pro_i em-o-tan-a-$ñ_i$

I *give-passive-pres-dec-1sg*

'I am given.'

(128b) pro_i em-ake-n-a-$ñ_i$

I *give-pst-VR/passive-dec-1sg*

'I was given.

The passive marker –o occurs in (128a) whereas the passive marker or verbal reflexive marker –n occurs in (128b) since they, sentence (128a) and (128b), are the present tense and the past tense markers respectively.

The reason as to why we need to compare the passive and the reflexive sentence in Ho is that both sentences are detransitivized.

---

[39] Both the passive marker and the reflexive marker in the present tense have a separate form from the intransitive maker *–n*. However, this is quite related with the position of the occurrence of direct object agreement marker in Ho. According to Koh (2002), in unmarked sentence the normal order is that subject agreement marker always occurs to the right of the preverbal word and object agreement marker occurs to the either left of the present tense marker or right of the past tense marker with respect to the [±animate].

Thus, both use the intransitive marker (both lack direct object): It is well known that the passivized verb loses the ability to assign structural accusative Case to its complement.

According to Ramamurti (1931: 26), Sora too, uses reflexive forms of verbs which express the meaning of the middle voice. It does not have the nominal anaphor but only has the verbal anaphor. Moreover, the verbal reflexive marker can also function as a passive marker. Thus, the verbal reflexive marker in Sora also shows the same pattern like Ho[40].

A sentence such as (128c) can have two interpretations: (i) The morpheme –n is treated as a verbal reflexive. Then it has the interpretation in (i). (ii) The morpheme –n is treaed as a passive morpheme. Then is has the interpretation in (ii).

(128c) (añ)$_i$ añ-te-ge-ñ$_i$ goe?-ke-n-a
I *me by emph 1sg* *kill pst [-TR] dec*
(i) 'I killed myself.'
(ii) 'I was killed by myself.'

In normal reflexive contexts in Ho, no direct objects occur except in some sentences as like (128d).

(128a) ram$_i$ kule-te-ge-?e$_i$ goe?-ke-n-a
Ram *tiger by emph 3sg* *kill pst [-TR] dec*
'? Ram KILLED HIS tiger.'
'Ram is killed by a tiger.'

When the direct object occurs with the postposition –te 'by' in reflexive sentences, it gets only a sloppy reading. Furthermore, this type of sentences can be interpreted as a passive too. But there is a difference between the two sentences: the PP, which occurs to the direct object position, kule 'tiger' is not identical with the subject añ 'I'

---

[40] Sora also belongs to the Austro-Asiatic language family. Let us consider the data from Sora.
pro$_i$ so: te-**n**-a'i$_i$
I *hide-fut-VR-dec-1sg*
i) 'I shall hide myself.'
ii) 'I will be hided.' (Ramamurti 1931)

in (128d) while the other PP, which also occurs to the same position, añ 'me' can be identical with the subject añ 'I' in (128c). Thus, (128d) is i) to stress the action as well as the possessive relationship (I claim that, in a sense, this is an indirect reflexivizing way of the subject's possession) since the intransitive marker (reflexive marker) is used, and the direct object occur as the PP, and ii) to show the passive since the intransitive marker (passive marker) and the PP occurs. Both sentences (128d) and (128c) are also the passive sentence and they have also a different interpretation.

Sentence (129) can be also interpreted as either the reciprocal or the passive. As shown in (129), we find the intransitive marker –n occurs in the reciprocal context. This also indicates that the reciprocal is also detransitivized in Ho. So, it has the interpretation of the passive due to the same morphological marker and the detransitiving effect.

(129) (ako)$_i$ Ø de-pe-ŋga-ke-n-a-ko$_i$

they *help-Recip-help pst [-tr] dec 3pl*

'They helped each other.'

'They were helped (by each other(?)).'

Let us look at (130) and (131).

(130) pro$_i$ ema-aka-n-a-ñ$_i$

I *give pres.perf [-tr] dec 1sg*

'I was given.'

'I have given myself.' (Burrows 1915)

(131) pro$_i$ Ø siŋboŋga-ta?a-re-m$_i$ ema-ke-n-a

you *God to in 2sg give pst [-TR/VR] dec*

i)'You gave yourself to the God.'

ii)'You were given to the God.'

We may ask how the intransitive marker -n can be used as the passive and the reflexive in Ho. It is enough to say that both are simply detransitivized.

In a sense, semantically, the meaning of the passive is very similar with the meaning of the reflexive as shown in (130) and (131). Who was dedicated to the God? That is 'I' or 'you' in both contexts. And the direct object agreement marker never occurs in both sentences due to the deransitivizing effect. This detransitivizing effect is also found in the causative constructions when the direct object and the subject are identical.

36. Vebal reflexive

Lidz (1996) says that the reflexive morpheme could represent some property of the syntax-semantics interface which cannot be unified in either of the other domains. There is some variation with respect to the uses of verbal reflexives (Lidz 1996:74): Many languages use the same morpheme for antipassive constructions as they use for reflexive construction. Middles are often represented by the same morpheme as reflexives, and impersonal sentences commonly mark the verb with the reflexive-marker. Papangeli (2001) also shows that Greek uses the same morpheme to mark reflexives, reciprocals, passives, (some) unaccusatives and middles. Further, it is a suffix that must be generated on the verb. Hence, it can only absorb the accusative case in Greek (Papangeli 2001). The reason as to why we need to compare the passive and the reflexive sentence in Ho is that both sentences are detransitivized. Thus, both use the intransitive marker (both lack the direct object). It is well known that the passivized verb loses the ability to assign structural accusative Case to its complement.

Let us look at sentences (132a) and (132b) where transitive verb goe? 'kill' carries the [-transitive] marker –n. The [-transitive] marker is in bold.

(132a) ram$_i$ kule-te-ge-$^?$e$_i$ goe$^?$-ke-**n**-a

Ram tiger by emph 3sg kill pst [-tr] dec

'? Ram KILLED HIS tiger.'

'Ram is killed by a tiger.'

(132b) (añ)$_i$ añ-te-ge-ñ$_i$ goe$^?$-ke-**n**-a

I me by emph 1sg kill pst [-tr] dec

'I killed myself.'

'I was killed by myself.'

As observed earlier, sentence (132b) gets only a sloppy reading. Moreover, this type of sentence can be interpreted as a passive too. But there is a difference between (132a) and (132b). The PP, which occurs in the canonical direct object position (A-position), kule 'tiger' is not identical with the subject añ 'I' in (132a) while the PP, which also occurs in the direct object position in (132b), añ 'me' is identical with the subject añ 'I'. Thus, (132a) is i) to stress the action as well as the possessive relationship since the intransitive marker –n (reflexive marker) is used, and the direct object occur as the PP, and ii) to show the passive since the intransitive marker –n (passive marker) and the PP occur. However, sentence (132b) does not stress action as well as the possessive relationship.

According to Haegeman (1994), in the passive sentence, the agent of the activity is not expressed by an NP in an A-position. If we wish to refer to the AGENT of the action, we need to use an adjunct PP headed by the preposition by, which itself carries the notion of AGENTIVITY. The thematic role of the subject añ 'I' can be both AGENT in (132a) and PATIENT in (132b) in the reflexive and the passive context respectively. The adjunct PP headed by the postposition –te 'by', añ-te-ge 'by me' or 'by myself', is the AGENT in the passive. Hence, in the normal meaning the STATUE interpretation in (132b) cannot be the Agent since the PP is not inanimate (the specific pronominal for 'I' is used: it cannot be interpreted as the 'statue', and [±animate] is quite an important factor in Ho and, to a great extent, the pronominal añ 'I' cannot be referred to the statue). So, the interpretation like 'I was killed by the statue' is not possible.

According to Lidz (2001), verbal reflexives are Pure-reflexives since they get only a sloppy reading. But the reflexive in Ho, which has only a verbal device but not the nominal device, gets both sloppy reading and strict reading although it is lexically reflexive marked. If so, why? The plausible solution is that the form of the reflexive and the passive is the same in past tense, that is -n as seen in (132a) and (132b). However, we get different interpretation of the marker –n in (132a) and (132b). This is because the direct object is pro in the unmarked reflexive sentences.

(133) pro$_i$ Ø goe$^?$-ke-n-a-ñ$_i$

I *kill pst VR dec 1sg*

'I killed myself (= myself or statue).'

'I was killed.'

Sentence (133) above can be interpreted as either a passive or a sentence with a reflexive due to the presence of the morphological marker –n. In the passive context, it does not show the Agent. Thus, the Patient pro which is añ 'I' in (133) is killed by someone or something. In case of the Madmae Tussaud context discussed in

Jackendoff (1992), however, the Agent can be either 'myself' or 'the statue'. Imagine that I go to the wax museum, which contains a statue of mine. On seeing the statue, I get frightened to death because the statue looks like a devil. I suddenly faint and die. In this situation the native speaker may say sentence (133) but not sentence (132b). If so, then why does sentence (133) get both readings in the reflexive context? This is because the direct object is pro, it is añ-te-ge-ñ 'I-by-emph-1sg' occurs in the canonical direct position in (133) whereas in sentence (132b), it is not. Furthermore, the property of this empty direct object is not due to pro-drop. The null object in (133) can refer to either añ 'me, myself' or the statue in (133) since pro has the property of [+R].

Sentence (134) can also be interpreted as either the reciprocal or the passive. It has the interpretation of the passive due to the occurrence of the same morphological marker and the marker also has detransitiving effect.

(134) (ako)$_i$ Ø de-pe-ŋga-ke-n-a-ko$_i$
they *help-Recip-help pst [-tr] dec 3pl*
'They helped each other.'
'They were helped (by each other(?)).'

Sentence (135) is interpreted as both the passive and the reflexive in Ho. Is it enough to say that both in (134) and (135) the marker –n detransitivize the verb?

(135) pro$_i$ ema-aka-n-a-ñ$_i$
I *give pres.perf [-tr] dec 1sg*
'I was given.'
'I have given myself.' (Burrows 1980)

The causative construction in Ho will shed some light on this issue. There is no monomorphemic word that corresponds to the English word 'show' in Ho. So, they use the causative construction as seen in (136a).

(136a) pro$_i$ kubiraj- ta$^?$a-re-ñ$_i$ Ø nel –ici -ke -n-a
I *doctor -to-in-1sg* *see –causative-pst-VR-dec*
'I showed myself to a doctor.'

(136b) ram$_i$ añ- ta$^?$a-ete-e$_i$ Ø giti-ici-ke-n-a

Ram me-to-by-3sg sleep-causative-pst-VR-dec

'Ram made me put himself to sleep.'

In (136a) and (136b), no direct object can occur since both sentences are detransitivized by the verbal reflexive marker. Instead, only NPs which are headed by the postposition can occur, but these PPs are not identical with the subject.

In imperative constructions, the subject is always in the second person. The suffix –me is the agreement marker of 2nd singular. Thus, the direct object is only identified with the 2nd person in the imperative reflexive contexts. In (137a), the verbal reflexive indicates that the direct object is coindexed with the subject which is 'you' in imperative constructions. In (137b), the direct object agreement marker –e occurs on the verb since the verbal reflexive does not occur.

(137a) pro$_i$ goe? –n$_i$ –me

kill –VR-imperative

'Kill yourself.'

(137b) kitab$_i$ ema-e$_i$-me

book give –3sg-imperative

'Give a book (to someone).'

Sentence (137c) is ungrammatical because the verbal reflexive is coindexed with the indirect object.

(137c) * kitab$_i$ ema-e$_i$-n-me

book give-3sg-VR-imperative

'Give a book to yourself.'

(137d) kitab ema-ko-me

book give-3pl-imperative

'Give a book to them.' (Deeney 1966)

As illustrated in (137c), it cannot be identical with the indirect object. Because. The verbal reflexive has the property of subject orientation. But, when there is an intervening NP, mostly a direct object in the reflexive context, the verbal reflexive cannot be identical with the subject and the passive interpretation is not available in Ho. The only possible interpretation is that is has the action stressing and possessive relationship as shown in (138a).

(138a) $añ_i$ $ciTTi\text{-}ñ_i$ ool-la-**n**-a

I *letter* *write-pst.perf-VR-dec*

'* I wrote a letter to myself.'

' I WROTE MY letter.'

'* I was written by a letter.'

The verbal reflexive cannot refer to the indirect object as in (137c) and (138a). The verbal reflexive is subject-oriented in Ho just as it is Dravidian (Subbarao and Lalita, Murthy 2000). Apart from the identity, the emphatic reflexive is used with the pronominal as illustrated in (138b).

(138b) $siŋboŋga_i$ pro_j $a^{y}e\text{-}lageD\text{-}ge^{?}\text{-}e_i$ bai-ke-D-$\mathbf{iñ}_j$-^{y}a

God *me* *him-for-emph-3sg* *creat pst [+TR] 1sg dec*

'The god created me for him/himself.'

However, the verbal reflexive marker/the intransitive marker cannot occur in such contexts. Instead, the transitive marker –D occurs. So, the direct object marker –iñ has to occur on the verb in (138b).

In many languages, the form of the verbal reflexive marker and the self-benefactive marker is homophonous. For example, it is kon in Telugu (Subbarao and Lalita Murthy 2000). Ho also has the same morphological form as shown in (139).

(139) añ-yo-ñ susun –ke –**n** –a

I-emph-1sg *dance-pst-self.ben-dec*

'I was danced.'

'I danced for myself.'

It is also significant to see the nature of pronominals and simplex anaphors in terms of reading property. This is because while Reinhart & Reuland group pronouns and SE anaphors (pure-reflexives) together in terms of internal structure, Lidz argues that pronominals and near-reflexives form a group together since they do not have semantic reflexivity. Let us examine which approach can be better for Ho? Let us consider the sentences (140) and (141) which are repeated here:

(140) pro$_i$ Ø$_i$ nel-ke -**n** -a -ñ$_i$

I *see-pst-VR-dec-1sg*

'I saw myself (= I or statue).'

(141) pro$_i$ añ$_i$ –te -ge -ñ$_i$ nel –ke -**n**-a

I *me-by-emph-1sg* *see-pst-VR-dec*

'I saw myself (= I, *statue).'

General idea about the Ho people

They are concentrated in the Kolhan area of the Singhbhum district of Jharkhand, and are also distributed in the adjacent areas of Orissa and West Bengal. They were once known as the Kol and Larka Kol. The name, Ho, is merely a 'contracted form of the word *horo*, or man' which is used by the cognate tribes of Munda and Santhal as their national designation. Their population in Jharkhand, Orissa, Chattisgarh, Bihar, according to the 2001 census, is 1,020,0000. They have a sex-ratio of 1026 females per 1000 males, and 6.78 percent of their total population is returned from urban areas. According to Risley, the Ho language was classed for linguistic purposes as the Munda or Kolarian. Now this mother tongue Ho is regarded as belonging to the Kherwarian group of the Austro-Asiatic family of languages. The Hindi language and the Devanagari script are used for inter-group communication. Those who reside in West Bengal use the Bengali language and Bengali script for inter-group communication. At the same time, the Ho from Oriya state is conversant with Hindi and uses the Oriya script. According to the 1961 census, 648,066 persons spoke the Ho language, of whom 141,856 persons were bilingual. Among the bilingual, 91,611 person (64.58 percent) spoken in Oriya as their second language, 44,242 person (31.19 percent) spoke in Hindi language while only 6003 persons(4.23 percent) spoke other languages as their second language. In the 1981 census 536,523 persons were returned as Ho language speakers, which show a rise of ethno-linguistic identity. Now, total number of people speaking the Ho language was 1,077,000 in 1997. As per the 2001 census, Hos have an overall literacy rate of 39.2% and a female literacy rate of 23.9%. This is against the overall literacy rate of 53.56% in Jharkhand, and a women's literacy rate of 38.87% in Jharkhand. Both are amongst the lowest literacy rates in India.

The Ho in general seem to be physically superior to many other tribal communities in Mayurbhanj. Usually, they are dark-brown in complexion with brown eyes. They have long black, straight or wavy hair. Among the men, the beard is scanty. The average height of an adult male is around 5'6" while that of the female is about 5'2". Dr. Haddon had added in case of the Ho of Singbhum that " They are dolicocephalic (C.I 74.5-76.0) with a long narrow forehead, irregular features, thick lips, eyes often bright and full and not oblique and the nose broad and flat-thus all are platyrrhine". The muscular physique and broad chest development among the men was attributed to : " The constant early use of the bow expanded the chest and set the muscles and their innate passion for the chase over the steep and rugged hills brought their lower limbs into a state of training which the best *phulwan*(wrestler0 of the plains of India might envy "

Although these generalized physical characters are often associated with the Ho, in reality one can find a variety of features due to constant racial admixture, especially with the Aryan blood. In spite of the fact that the Larka Kol had exhibited utmost military skill and aggressiveness during the British days, and their well-built feature may immediately give the impression of toughness, they are found to be extremely hospitable and sober, once the stranger gains the confidence of the community.

Starting from the period between the 9th and 12th centuries, copper was smelted in many parts of old Singhbhum district. It is believed that many immigrants entered Singhbhum from Manbhum in the 14th century or earlier. When the Hos entered old Singhbhum, they overcame the Bhuiyas, who were then inhabitants of the forest country. In the latter half of the eighteenth century, the Hos fought several wars against the Rajas of Chota Nagpur and Mayurbhanj to retain their independence. As far as is known, the Muslims left them alone. The area was formally claimed to be a part of the Mughal Empire, neither the Mughals nor the Marathas, who were active in the surrounding areas during the decline of the Mughals, ventured into the area.

In 1765, Chota Nagpur was ceded to the British East India Company as part of Bengal, Bihar and Orissa. The Raja of Singhbhum asked the British Resident at Midnapore for protection in 1767 but it was not until 1820 that he acknowledged himself as a feudatory of the British. The restless Hos broke the agreement soon and took part in the fierce rebellion of 1831-33, along with the Mundas. The immediate cause of the Kol uprising in 1831-32 was the oppression of Adivsis by non-Adivasi thikadars (literally meaning contractors) or farmers of rent. The Hos and Mundas were joined by the Oraons and the houses of many dikku (non-Adivasis or outsiders) landlords were burnt and a number of people were killed. It compelled the British to recognise a thorough subjugation of the Hos. The uprising was suppressed with a good deal of trouble by Captain Wilkinson, who had several hundred troops at his disposal. While local troops quelled the uprising, another group under Colonel Richards entered Singhbhum in November 1836. Within three months all the headmen surrendered. In 1857, the Raja of Porahat rose in rebellion and a sizable section of the Hos joined in the revolt. Troops were sent and that put an end to the disturbances in 1859.

Land is their main economic resource which is controlled individually. Forests and water are the other economic resources. The Ho are mainly a landowning community and are primarily engaged in agriculture. They sell firewood, collect forest produce, fish occasionally and sell rice beer. It is also observed from the census returns that of the total population, the workers constitute 38.67 percent as agricultural laborers and 7.40 percent as engaged in manufacturing, processing, serving, etc. The remaining 8.21 percent are distributed in various other occupations.

The Ho follows traditional tribal religion and their sacred specialists are from their own community. They celebrate festivals like Maghe Parab, Henro Parab, Jomnama Bahtuali and Baha. The 1981 census returns 81.65 percent of the Ho under 'other religions' showing a majority of their population as followers of a tribal religion. Of the rest, 16.52 percent are Hindus, 1.43 percent are Christians, and the rest are Muslims, Sikhs and those who have not stated their religion. A comparison of the 1961-81 census data shows that there has been an increase in the number of the people who follow their own traditional tribal religion from 73.30 percent in 1961 to 77.30 percent in 1971, which future increased to 81.65 percent in 1981. The persons who profess Hinduism declined from 26.15 percent on 1961 to 21.46 percent in 1971, and further declined to 16.52 percent in the 1981 census. The Christians are on the increase among them from 0.55 percent in 1961 to 1.15 percent in 1971, and have further declined to 1.43 percent in 1981.

The Ho once participated in the Kol rebellion, and nowadays some of them are involved in the Jharkhand Movement. The art and craft of the community are wall painting and mat-weaving. Their musical instruments are percussion and wind types. Both men and women take part in folk-songs and dances.

The Ho maintains economic relations with local artisans, and service and agricultural communities. These days some of the Ho works as industrial laborers and also hold jobs in different organized sectors. The self-employed persons among them are tailors or run poulthy farms. Quite a few of the Ho boys and girls have studied upto the college and university level. According to the 1981 census, in Bihar, 17.71 percent of them are returned literate. The male and female literacy rates are 29.30 and 6.41 percent, respectively. They use both modern and traditional medicine and have a favorable attitude towards the family planning program. They have benefited from employment generation schemes. The radio is the medium of communication. Wood and cow-dung cakes are the sources of fuel. They use chemical fertilizers and insecticides in their fields.

The Ho, inhabiting the state of Orissa, migrated fron the Lolhan region, which is now on the Singbhum district of Jharkhand. They are divided into various groups like the Chao, Birwar, Rarnganjia, Kolhan, etc. They are also called Kolha. In Orissa they are distributed in Cuttacl, Kalahandi, Dhenkanal, Keonhjhargarh, Mayurbhanj and some other districts, and number 44,496 persons (1981). They have a number of exogamous clans (kili) such as Hembrom, Tiria, Pingua, Jamuda, Samad, Danga and Hansda. Clan names and sometimes names such as Naik and Singh are used as surnames, though marriage through negotiation is the common mode of acquiring mates, though marriage by symbolic capture, intrusion, exchange and mutual consent is also in vague. They also work as agricultural laborers, make ropes from sabui grass, and collect and sell forest produce and firewood. According to the 1981 census, 40.07 percent of them are returned as workers (57.04 percent males and 23.16 percent females). Among these works, 55.79 percent are returned as cultivators, 31.62 percent as agricultural laborers and 2.08 percent as engaged in forestry, hunting, etc. The remaining 10.51 percent of the workers are engaged on mining and quarrying, in the household industry, in transport and storage, etc. Though cash is their, main mode of transaction, puffed and parched rice are often bartered for paddy or rice.

The Ho follows a religion which is a mixture of their own tribal religion and Hinduism. The 1981 census returns 81.49 percent of the Go as followers of Ginduism, 0.87 percent as Christians and 3.70 percent as those who have not stated their religion. There has been a significant revival if tribal religion which is attested to by the fact that 13.94 percent of them have been returned under 'other religions'. A comparison of the 1961-81 census data shows that the population of Hindus is on the decline from 99.97 percent in 1961 to 86.76 percent in 1971 and further to 81.49 percent on 1981. In the 1971 census a good number of them, i.e. 12.79 percent, have been returned under 'other religions' which includes the tribe's traditional religion. They worship clan deities like Thakurani and Maranga-Bonga, village deities like Gram Sin, Baram and Basuki, regional deities like Basumata and Sing Bonga, and deities of the wider pantheon such as Lakshmi, Saraswati, etc. Their sacred specialists are the deheri, jyotish, Brahmin purohit, ojha, gunin and some more, who belong to their own and to the neighboring communities. The Ho are expert in body tattooing, and floor and wall drawing. Singing and dancing are an ontegral part of their lives. They have traditional intercommunity relations with peasants like the Mahato and Karan, artisans and serving people like the Kamar, Rajak and Napit. Their literacy rate is 21.93 and 3.61 percent, respectively.

The Ho ise also distributed in different parts of the Midnapur district of west Bengal. A few of them live on tea plantations. According to the 1981 census, their total population on West Bangal is 3202. They use Singh, Nayak, Chatar, Tiria, etc. As surnames, most of which are derived from the clan (gotra) names. It is believed that all the gotra originated from the god Marang Bonga. The vermillion mark and conch shell bangles are symbols of marriage for the women. The Ho who lives on West Bengal observes twenty-one days of birth pollution. Before marriage they worship the god Sing Bonga and sacrifice a fowl. The dead are cremated. They pursue agriculture, labor, rickshaw-pulling, and few more occupations for their subsistence. The workers account for 45.13 percent (55.23 percent males and 34.20 percent females) of their total population. A majority, i.e. 60.35 percent are returned as agricultural labourers. This is followed by 17.72 percent as cultivators, 12.73 percent in other-than-household industries and the remaining 9.20 percent in various other occupations. The 1981 census returns 97.69 percent of the Ho of West Bangal as followers of Hinduism, 0.87 percent as Christians, 0.22 percent as Muslims and 1.22 percent as those who profess 'other religions'. The 1961 and 1971 census returns do not show any significant change. The community has not made factory progress in the field of education. The literacy rate among the Ho is 11.62 percent. The sex-wise literacy rate shows that 18.39 percent of the males and 4.29 percent of the females are literate.

Like most other communities, the Ho strongly believes in supernatural beings and has faith on the soul of departed individuals. Both gods and goddesses are termed as *bonga* by the Ho, who regulates their day to day individual and communal behavior. Every *bonga* is feared for, as the slightest deviation in its propitiation may lead to irreparable damage to the entire village by the outbreak of epidemics or crop failure or death by wild animals etc. Ho gods and goddesses are non-anthropomorphic and are believed to hover around hills, forests, cultivated fields within the village premises. Of course, every Ho village has permanent abode for their *bongas*, which is usually a sal groove (jatira), a little away from the village, where regular sacrifice is offered to them. The spirits of dead ancestors normally take shelter inside the single-roomed house, where offerings are made in their honor no festive occasions. Ho *bongas* are divided into two types, such as, the benevolent and the malevolent, depending on their nature. Although no definite hierarchical order of the *bongas* is recognized by these Ho, there is a general consensus that '*sing bonga'* is the chief among all, who created the universe.

'*sing bonga'* among the Ho is otherwise called as '*dharamdebata*' or the sun god. He is believed to be omnipresent and hence, no definite place of worship is accorded to him. He is worshipped first at any festive occasion and the *dehuri* or the village priest sacrifices a chicken (*sim*) in his honor. Even in family worships, '*sing bonga'* is propitiated first and then the other gods or spirits, The Ho even swear in his name to express the truth and during any kind of give and take, with the belief that the god is the only witness for the transactions.

The religious sentiment and devotion to the *bongas* among the Ho culminate in a number of communal festivals, besides the domestic rituals. The Ho observe four major festivals which are communal in nature, and are combinations of socio-religious and recreational activities. These are : (1) *magh puri*, (2) *ba parab*, (3) *hera parab*, (4) *jamnam parab*

After the harvest, when the granaries are almost full, the Ho observe this festival during the month of January-February. The date is fixed in a joint meeting of the *dehuri* and elder members of the village. The festival is continued for six days and invariably followed by drinking and dancing, which facilitates choosing marital partners among the youth. These six days of celebration are named separately by the Ho :

1 st day : gawal	2 nd day : ate ili	3 rd day : sange ili
4 th day : marang-musing	5 th day : basi-musing	6 th day : har bagia

On the first day of the festival, there is no communal worship excepting that every household offers pooja to the ancestral spirits. Rice-beer is prepared for the purpose and ceremonial offering of rice, curry and rice-beer is made to the spirits. All members of the household, irrespective of age and sex, drink the rice-beer in the night. The house is cleaned with cow-dung water on this day.

The second day is the offering of ili or rice-beer to the bongas by the village priest. Every household head assembles at the residence of the dehuri with a pot of rice-beer. After the formal offering of rice-beer is made to the bongas, the villagers drink rice-beer as much as the can and dance.

On the third day, again the villagers wash their houses clean. The courtyard, granaries etc. are cleaned with cow-dung water. Even this solution is sprinkled over all the used materials like utensils. The people of the village do not attend to any work except drinking, dining and dancing.

The fourth day marks the real ritual part of the festival. A pandal is specially erected for the purpose outside the village. The pandal is decorated by the village youth. The priest along with the villagers comes to the pandal around the mid-day. The villagers bring a big pot of rice-beer. Chickens are procured for the purpose. The priest scatters sun-dried rice. It is regarded as auspicious, if the chickens swallow them. Then the sacrifice of these chickens is made to dessauli, gram siri, sing bonag etc. to protect the village. After the propitiation is over, the villagers, male and female, drink rice-beer and dance with obscene songs, narrating the male and female organs or inviting each other for sexual intercourse.

The fifth day is the day of bidding good-bye to the invited spirits. The village youth sing and dance.

On the sixth day, they beat the roof of every house in a group with the belief that this act expels all diseases, miseries from the village and brings in peace. They collect rice, vegetables etc. from every household and arrange a feast outside the village. The festival is unavoidable for any Ho village and any deviation to the observance invites only miseries to the villagers. In spite of this folk belief, the festival is otherwise thought to be recreational and smooth the process of selecting life partners.

The family is regarded as the smallest socio-economic-politico-religious unit among the Ho, like all other tribal and non-tribal communities. As usual, the nuclear family consists of the parents and their unmarried sons and daughters, while the joint family accommodates the married brothers and their children. Monogamy among the Ho is a common practice with rare occurrence of polygynous families. Although polygyny if never encouraged in a Ho community, it takes place in exceptional situations like the barren or disabled first wife. The supremacy of the first wife nevertheless is maintained and the second wife is only sought for with her approval. The father is recognized as the head of the family and all authorities relating to the overall maintenance of the family vested to him. He officiates in all the family rituals and represents the family in village functions.

Inter-personal relations perpetuates between the members of the family, which is based on cordiality, mutual love, affection and sympathy. Even when the married sisters are divorced by their husbands, they usually get back to the natal family and remain there either till the dispute is settled any way or they are remarried elsewhere.

As an economic unit, the family functions under the leadership of the father. The wife, besides her regular responsibilities of household works and child-care, assists the husband in agricultural operations and sometimes engaging herself as a daily wager to supplement the family income. Unmarried grown up daughters also contribute immensely to the family economy. Till his death, the father maintains his supremacy as the head of the family. After his death, all the movable and immovable properties are distributed among the sons and they get separated according to their respective convenience. The eldest son usually gets a little more landed property than his usual share, due to the fact that all family friends and relatives pay their visit to the residence of the eldest son in case of any family festival.

The typical Ho house has either one multi-purpose room or 2-3 rooms at the most. If it is a one-roomed house, it is partitioned to at least three small spaces by a temporary tin wall. One of these spaces is used as kitchen, while the other two are used for storing grains and for multi-purpose use. If the house has more than one room, every room is separate in its function. The doors are either wooden of bamboo, and windows are conspicuously absent in most of cases. The entrance of the house is ideally toward the east, although it is not strictly adhered to. The roof is thatched and mud floor is common. The walls are either bamboo-made or from a local variety of shrub, plastered with mud. The walls are painted with yellow or red mud, which are locally available.

Change is, perhaps inevitable for any society at any point of time and any any place. Hence the Ho society is exposed to the vagaries of modern forces of industrialization. Moreover Ho language is getting changed by the influence of Hindi which is officially spoken in Jharkhand as we have seen in the areal features of Ho. However the Ho people have been trying to keep their tradition including festivals, marriage ceremony, etc and keep Ho language. In fact they already created its own script by themselves though it is not written now.

REFERENCES

Asher, R.E. 1994. *The Encyclopedia of Language and Linguistics*. Oxford : Pergamon Press

Burrows, Lionel. 1915 (repr.1980). *The Grammar of the Ho Language*. New Delhi : Cosmo Publications.

Chomsky, N. 1995. *The minimalist program*. Massachusetts : The MIT Press

Chomsky, N. 1981. *Lectures on Government and Binding*. Dordrecht: Foris.

Cole, P & L-M. Sung. 1994. 'Head Movement and Long Distance Reflexives', *Linguistic Inquiry* 25: 355-406.

Cook, V and Newson, M. 1996. *Chomsky's Universal Grammar*. Oxford: Blackwell.

Crystal, D. 1991. *A Dictionary of Linguistics and Phonetics*. Oxford : Blackwell Publishers

Culicover, Peter. W. 1997. *Principles ad Parameters: An Introduction to Syntactic Theory*. New York: OUP.

Deeney, John. 1966. *An Introduction to the Ho language*. Bihar: Xavier Ho Publication.

Greenberg, Joseph H. 1963. *Universals of Languages*. Cambridge, Mass. : MIT Press.

Grierson, G. A. 1967. *Lingustic Survery of India*. Vol.Ⅸ Part 4. (Re-printed) Delhi : Motilal Banarasi Dass.

Grimshaw, Jane. 1990. *Argument Structure*. Cambridge: Mass. MIT Press.

Haegeman, Liliane. 1994. *Introduction to Government and Binding Theory*. Oxford: Blackwell Publishers Limited.

Harbert, W. 1995. Binding theory, Control, and pro, in Webelhuth, Gert. (ed.), *Government and Binding Theory and the Minimalist* Program. Oxford: Blackwell.

Jackendoff, Ray. 1983. *Semantics and Cognition*. Cambridge: Mass. MIT Press.

Jackendoff, Rav. 1990. *Semantic Structure. Cambridge*: Mass. MIT Press.

Jayaseelan, K. A. 1999. 'Reflexivizing a pronoun in Malayalam', in *Parametric studies in Malayalam syntax*. Mumbai: Allied Publisher Limited.

Jayaseelan, K. A. 1999. 'Malayalam anaphors and the binding principles', in *Parametric studies in Malayalam syntax*. Mumbai: Allied Publisher Limited.

K. K. Misra. 1987. *Social structure and change among the Ho of Orissa*. Delhi : Gian Publishing House

Lasnik, H. 1989. *Essasy on Anaphora*. Dordecht: Reidel.

Lidz, Jeffery. 1996. *Dimensions of Reflexivity*, Doctoral dissertation. Newark: University of Delaware.

Lidz, Jeffery, 2001. Condition R. *Linguistic Inquiry* 32:123-140.

Lust, B., Wali,K., Gair. J. & Subbarao, K. V. 2000. Lexical Anaphors and Pronouns in Selected South Asian Languages: *A Principled Typology*. New York: Mouton, de Gruyter.

Osada, T. 1992. *A reference grammer of Mundari*. Tokyo: Tokyo University of Foreign Studies.

Osada, T. Reciprocals in Mundari, in V.Nedjalkov and A. Guentcheva. (eds.), *Typological of reciprocal constructions*. Munich : Lincom Europa.

Papangeli, Dimitra. 2001. 'Greek reflexives and the issue of productivity' in Alexiadou, A., Anagonstopoulou, E. and M, Everaert. (eds.), *The Unaccusativity puzzle: Studies on the syntax-lexicon Interface*. Oxford: Oxford University Press.

Pustejovsky, James. 1991. 'The syntax of event structure', in Beth Levin and Steven Pinker. (eds.), *Lexical and Conceptual Semantics*. Cambridge: Blackwell.

Raamurti,G.V. & Rao,S. 1931. *A manual of the sora(or savara) language*. Madras: the superintendent, Government press.

Reinhart, Tanya. 1983. *Anaphora and Semantic Interpretation*. London : Croom Helm.

Reinhart, T. & Siloni, T. 1999. 'Against the Unaccusative Analysis of Reflexives', in Alexiadou, A., Anagonstopoulou, E. and M. Everaert. (eds.), *The Unaccusativity puzzle: Studies on the syntax-lexicon Interface*. Oxford: Oxford University Press.

Reinhart, T. and Reuland, E. 1993. Reflexivity. *Linguistic Inquiry* 24, 657-720.

Reuland, E. 2001. Primitives of Binding. *Linguistics Inquiry* 31.

Rizzi, L. 1986. Null objects in Italian and the theory of pro. *Linguistics Inquiry* 17, 501-58.

Subbarao, K. V. 1999. Languages Universals and Syntactic Typology: A proposal for a Symbiotic Relationship, in Rajendra Singh, (ed.), *The yearbook of South Asian Languages and Linguistics*. New Delhi: Sage.

Subbarao, K. V. 2001. 'Agreement in South Asian Languages': A paper delivered at the lecture. Delhi: University of Delhi.

Subbarao, K. V. 2001. Syntactic Typological and South Asian Languages, in Rajendra Singh, (ed.), *The Yearbook of South Asian Languages and Linguistics. New Delhi: Sage.*

Subbarao, K. V. 2001. 'pro-DROP, Agreement and Argument Structure': Plenary lecture delivered at the SALA conference. Konstanz: University of Konstanz.

Tae-Jin, Koh. 2002. *Agreement in Ho*: M.A. disseration. Delhi: University of Delhi.

Witzel, Michael, 1999, 'Substrate Languages in Old Indo-Aryan (□gvedic, Middle and Late Vedic).' Electronic Journal of Vedic Studies 5 (1).

About the Author Dr. Koh, Tae-Jin was educated at the Hankuk University of Foreign Studies and University of Delhi. He obtained B.A. in Hindi, M.A., M.Phil., and Ph.D in Linguistics. He currently teaches Hindi at the Hankuk University of Foreign Studies and Pusan University of Foreign Studies.

A TYPOLOGICAL GRAMMAR OF HO

First printed May. 11. 2009.
First published May. 20. 2009.
The writer Koh, Tae-Jin
The publisher Park, Chul
Hankuk University of Foreign Studies Press
270 Imun-dong Dongdaemun-gu, Seoul, 130-791
Tel : 82-2-2173-2495~6
Fax : 82-2-2173-3363
Homepage : http://press.hufs.ac.kr
e-mail : press@hufs.ac.kr
Registration of publisher : 6-6(Apr. 30. 1969)

ISBN 978-89-7464-545-8 93790 ₩18,000